Books by Margaret S. Ernst

IN A WORD
(1939)

drawings by
James Thurber

A book for young people
WORDS
(1937, 1950)

These are BORZOI BOOKS
published by
Alfred A. Knopf
in New York

More about Words

MARGARET S. ERNST

More about

Words

Sketches by W. A. DWIGGINS

1966 *NEW YORK* ALFRED A. KNOPF

THIS IS A BORZOI BOOK,
PUBLISHED BY ALFRED A. KNOPF, INC.

PUBLISHED APRIL 23, 1951
SECOND PRINTING, SEPTEMBER 1962
THIRD PRINTING, DECEMBER 1964
FOURTH PRINTING, JULY 1966

Foreword

More about Words is a kind of random dictionary of some thousand bits of the English language whose curious origins just happened to entrance me. It is not a book for the serious philologist but rather for those people who, like me, relish words and their changing histories, who think words are fun, and who may, using my book as a springboard, swim along in the peaceable currents of the dictionary.

The amateur of words, in the strict sense of *amateur* (derived from Latin "lover"), will find here much of history and biography; a feeling of how language changes as the mores change; poetry; and a lot of humor. A dentist of my acquaintance keeps a copy of my previous book, *In a Word*, on his waiting-room table, and he tells me it is the perfect reading-matter for a doctor's antechamber— you can pick it up anywhere, put it down anywhere, and it brings the victim in smiling.

The words are arranged as in a dictionary, but one word always reminds me of another, so there is no orderly sequence. It is like rantumscooting on Nantucket Island, where, in driving over the moors, one sandy rutted track leads into another, and that into still another in a contrary direction.

In spite of this light-hearted approach to the thesaurus (derived from "treasure-house") of English language, I believe this collection will be a stimulus to students of words, and it is, to the best of my ability, correct in its scholarship. I have drawn most of my material from such solid sources as the Oxford *New English Dictionary*, old Skeat, the fascinating books of Ernest Weekley and Mencken, other dictionaries and encyclopedias. Where I rely on folk etymology, I honestly say so. The critics of my first book taught me caution, and I am ruefully grateful to them. I am also grateful to the readers of *In a Word* who wrote hundreds of letters, sometimes making me a present of a new etymology, sometimes setting me to rights. Thanks, too, to Paula Gross, who typed the book without any apparent boredom.

More about Words

aberration

This word comes from the Latin verb *aberrare*, to wander off. A mental *aberration* is a straying away from the recognized path of normal thinking; hence, to the conventional and orthodox, moral irregularity. *Erratic, err, erratum*, and *erroneous* are from the same Latin stem. Tennyson, in "Gareth and Lynette," uses *error* in this literal sense of "off the track": "The damsel's headlong error through the wood."

Errant, as in *knight-errant*—a chivalrous fellow on a mission—is the result of a fusion of two sources: Latin *iterare*, to journey, has become entangled with *errare*, to stray.

Arrant started its etymological life as a variant of *errant*, but by constant association with "thief" or "rogue" or "knave" lost its original sense, and came to mean notorious, unmitigated; outright wicked. An early case of guilt by association. Chaucer has a line about "a thief errant."

abet

In both legal and general use, *abet* means to incite, instigate, or encourage someone to go ahead and act, and damn the consequences. Rarely are people aided and *abetted* in virtue; for some reason, the *abetment* is generally in the direction of crime, major or minor.

In old French, *à beter* meant to bait, to hound on, as in hunting; its probable earlier source was Norse *beita*, to cause to bite. After the Norman Conquest, and particularly in the 14th and 15th centuries, bear-baiting was almost as popular in England as cricket is today. The starved and not unnaturally vicious beast was put in a pit with enthusiastic dogs, to fight to the finish. The dogs' owners and the spectators *abetted* them with cries of "Go it, Fido," or the Middle English equivalent.

Bet, in the sense of a wager or to wager, is the same word, probably, though the sense development is obscure. Was it, originally, to *bet* money on a champion? Or was it to *bet* (i.e., *abet*) a champion with money? *You bet*, as in Groucho Marx's radio program "You Bet Your Life," is U.S. slang and a synonym for "certainly."

abeyance

This word comes to us from Late Latin *badare*, meaning to open the mouth wide, to gape. A person "held in abeyance" would stand goggling, with dropped jaw, waiting in suspense for a miracle, or at any rate for something surprising. We, however, make use of the figurative sense of the word only, to denote a state of suspension, temporary inactivity, a dormant condition liable to be disturbed at any moment.

In law, the phrase "held in abeyance" connotes an undetermined condition, as of an estate in search of an owner.

One conjecture as to the origin of the Latin stem is that it developed from the elementary sound "ba," made when the mouth, of either men or sheep, drops open involuntarily. If this is true, the *bay* of a hound on the hunting trail has the same derivation.

abominate

From Latin *abominor*, meaning "I pray that the omen may be averted." The Romans muttered this word when they mentioned anything unlucky, just as we knock on wood to frighten away jealous spirits. In Latin, *ab* means away; *omen*, good or evil sign or portend. An *abominable* sight is one exciting disgust; odious, detestable. The men of the Middle Ages spelled it *abhominable* and thought the word derived from "away from man" (*homo*), therefore, inhuman, beastly.

abracadabra

Latin, of unknown origin, this cabalistic word occurs first in a poem by Quintus Severus Sammonicus in the 2nd century, and was used as a charm. The Romans believed it had the power to cure agues, toothache, and other ills. (Early psychosomatic medicine.) The patient wrote the letters in a triangular arrangement on parchment that was hung around the neck on linen thread. Then he waited.

We use *abracadabra* as a pretended conjuring word, or to express contempt for some politician's would-be spell-binding.

That *Abracadabra* was the supreme deity of the Assyrians is unauthenticated.

accumulate

From the Latin *accumulare*, to heap up. When you *accumulate* wealth, you pile it up, heap it up by additions of sturdy sums. In 1533 More wrote to Henry VIII: "Of your mere abundant goodness heped and accumilate upon me." *Cumulus* clouds are those vast, heaped-up billows you see in the summer sky.

adieu

The French expression *à Dieu* means "to God." This is an abbreviation of the sentence *"Je vous recommande à Dieu,"* "I commend you to God," said between friends on parting.

"God be with ye" was contracted to our familiar and not at all religious *good-bye. Adieu* is a farewell for a longer time than *au revoir,* which is French for "until I see you again."

admiral

This is an artificial spelling of the French *amiral*. The oldest sense, in both French and English, is *emir*, a Saracen chief. The Arabian word *amir*, commander, is commonly followed by *al*, as in *amir-al-bahr*, commander of the sea, from which a clipped noun *amiral* resulted. The Arabs in Spain called their highest naval officer "amir-al-bahr" or "amir-al-ma," from which we get our Lord High Admiral. A mistaken 16th century etymologist referred to Columbus as *admirans mare*, meaning "admiring the sea" —which he undoubtedly didn't, on those endless voyages. *Admire* is from an entirely different root, Latin "to wonder at," from *mirus*, wonderful. *Marvel* and *miracle* come from this source.

One for the entomologist rather than the etymologist: the *admiral butterfly* wears scarlet and white stripes on his uniform.

adore

This religious word, from Latin *adorare*, to pray to, has become secularized to such an extent that we *adore* a new perfume, or find a baby *adorable*.

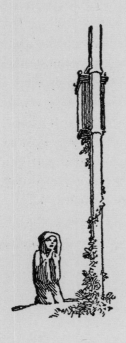

aloof

This disinterested word, which we use figuratively, as Hamlet did ("I stand aloofe, and will no reconcilement"), was originally a sailor's term: *a loof*, to the luff or windward direction, perhaps from the Dutch *te loef*, to windward. The original meaning of the Dutch word and its connection with Middle English *lof, loof*, some kind of rudder or steering apparatus, are not clear. From the idea of keeping a ship's head to the wind, and thus clear of the lee shore toward which she might drift, came the general sense of steering clear of, or giving a wide berth to anything threatening, with which one might come into collision unless one stood *aloof*.

Luff: to sail nearer the wind so that the sail flutters. In Young's Nautical Dictionary, 1846, we find: "The weather part of a fore-and-aft sail . . . the side next the mast or stay to which it is attached." Our family sloop *Episode* occasionally *luffs*, but, being a friendly lady, is never *aloof*. *Episode's* attendant dink is named the *Incident*, which might be defined as a very small episode. *Episode* comes from the Greek, and was originally that part of a Greek tragedy interpolated between two choric songs. We get *incident* from the Latin *incidere*, to fall in; hence, an unexpected or untoward happening. *Dink* is affectionate for *dinghy*, in Hindu *dingi*, a small boat hollowed out of a log, like an Indian dugout.

amazon

From Greek *a mazos*, without a breast. Nowadays, any outsize or intimidating woman—the Thurber predatory female, for example—is an *amazon*; but, according to legend, the *Amazons*, the "Breastless," were deadly efficient warrior-women who lived near the Euxine. In order to have nothing interfere with their bows (weapons, not frills), they cut off their right breasts. They were allies of the Trojans against the Greeks, and their queen, Penthesilea, was killed by Achilles.

The king of Dahomey, in West Africa, led a band of *amazons* against the French in 1894. And a kind of ant that carries off and enslaves the young of another species is the *Amazon ant*.

The great river of South America was given the name *Amazonas* by the Spanish explorer Orellana, in 1541, after a battle with the Tapuyas savages in which the women of the tribe fought alongside the men.

ambassador

In Cæsar's *Gallic War*, this is the word he uses to designate a vassal or retainer of a Gallic chief. Some etymologists believe the word came into English, via French *ambassadeur*, from *embactiare*, to go about on a mission. Other authorities believe it derives from a fusion of the Latin *ambi-*, around, about, both ways, and the Celtish Breton word *aketuz*, busy; hence, an *ambassador* was a retainer employed about his lord, or sent on a mission by him. An *ambassador of good will*, employed about his President's business, has his hands full these days of the chill war.

In the 17th and 18th centuries, the popular spelling was "embassador," whence our *embassy*.

ambiguous

This is one of several words growing on the Latin stem *ambus*, meaning both, on both sides. This comes from *ambigere*, to drive both ways at once, a difficult feat. *Ambiguous* remarks are those which go in several confusing directions at once, leaving the listener in considerable doubt as to their meaning.

Ambidextrous means able to use both hands alike. In Latin, *dexter* is the right hand, *sinister* the left; a patent libel on left-handed people, who no doubt once took their enemies by surprise with a left-handed or southpaw rapier job; sinister business.

Ambit comes from *ambire*, to go about, a compass, a circle, a circumference; and *ambition* has exactly the same derivation. The *ambitious* Roman citizen went around in his white toga—whence our *candidate*, since *candid* means white—canvassing for votes. Times have not changed, except for the costume.

amnesty

From the Greek *amnaomai*, not to remember. When the ruling authority grants an *amnesty* he is not remembering past offenses, he is forgetting faults. *Amnestia* is the Law of Oblivion. A man who forgets who he is or where he lives suffers from *amnesia*.

Mnemonics is one of those trick systems for remembering —for example, "vibgyor" is the code word for the colors of the rainbow: violet, indigo, blue, green, yellow, orange, red.

Another word for forget is *oblivion*, from Latin *oblivisci*, to forget, from *oblivere*, to be black and blue, dark. In a state of *oblivion* is to be in the dark. *Livid*, from the same root, means discolored, black and blue, as from a bruise. *Livid* with anger: your face becomes blue; a *livid* sky in a storm is bruised with dark clouds.

ancillary

This term, usually met with in highly technical documents such as insurance policies, wills, and other legal briefs, referring to subordinate clauses, literally means subservient, ministering, pertaining to a handmaiden. *Ancilla* is Latin for handmaid, diminutive of *ancus, anca,* servant. Thackeray, in *Henry Esmond,* used the word in its literal sense: "The ancillary beauty was the one whom the Prince had selected."

anemone

This delightful spring flower is named for *Anemone*, daughter of the wind, from *anemos*, the wind. Tennyson, in his *A Dream of Fair Women*, wrote:

> *And at the root thro' lush green grasses burn'd*
> *The red anemone.*

Anemocracy means government by the winds, a term that might apply to modern France with its frequent changes of ministry.

An instrument for measuring the velocity of the wind is called an *anemometer*.

animal

This is a Latin word meaning anything living, from *anima*, air, breath of life. We humans are equally *animals* with the breathers in the zoo. The word was not known in English till the end of the 16th century, and is not found in the 1611 Bible as a synonym for beasts.

From the same stem we get *animadvert*, meaning to turn the mind toward someone or something. This word, at first meaning consideration of a subject, now means hostile attention or criticism, a turning against.

In a Disney cartoon, you see credit given to the *animators*. This is a precise use of the word, as *animate* means, literally, to fill with breath or life.

Animosity originally meant high spirit, courage. Since high spirits were frequently hot-tempered, the word gradually took on the heat of hostility. In the same way, *animus* changed from soul, mind, passion to a feeling of a hostile character. A *magnanimous* person is great-spirited.

A 1

This expression for anything excellent, first-class, was originally used in *Lloyd's Register*, in London, in its rating of ships and its estimate of their insurance risk. Dickens in 1837 used the term about persons and things. The United States form became A *No. 1*. Variants were: A *1 copper-bottomed*; A *1 at Lloyd's*. The origin is obvious, A being at the top of the batting order in the alphabet, 1 in numerals.

artifice

This word, from the Latin *artificium*, to make or create art, originally meant just what it says—to make something through skilled workmanship or craft. It has now taken on the sense of human skill as opposed to "doing what comes naturally," and, human beings being as they sometimes are, the further sense of cunning and trickery. *Artificial* flowers are made of paper or cloth or maybe nylon, not grown in a garden. Sir Thomas Browne in 1646 said: "Adam immediately issued from the Artifice of God."

atom

The atom bomb is the nightmare of the 20th century, and atomic energy is its hope of salvation, according to David Lilienthal. But the origins of this small, round word held no special threat or promise. It is from Latin *atomus*, the twinkling of an eye (the shortest measure of time) and from Greek *atemno*, not cut, indivisible, something so small it cannot be divided. In medieval times, an *atom* was the smallest measure of time, $15\frac{5}{94}$ths of a second.

We have *atomizers* for perfume on our dressing-tables.

atone

This is short for the adverbial phrase "set or make at one." (As late as the 16th century "one" was pronounced "own.") From Latin *unire*, make one, unite, put at one, this verb at first had no implication of making amends for wrong deeds done, and meant simply to set at one, "onement," agreement. We had originally the verb "to one." In those days, a proposal of marriage might have been: "Will you one with me?" Milton wrote: "The King and parliament will soon be attoned."

Related words are *once*, *union*, and *onion*, a vegetable whose many skins are wrapped into one, just as the members of a union are, collectively, one.

austere

From Greek *austeros* dry, making the tongue dry and rough. What happens in England today under Sir Stafford Cripps's Austerity Program, with all the Scotch shipped to the U.S.A. Evelyn wrote, in 1664 in *Pomona*, of "Austere fruit." From meaning "dry," *austere* has come to be harsh, stern, severe, grim, severely unadorned in style, without any luxury.

Auster is the south wind, a dry, kindling wind. *Australia* is from Latin *terra australis*, southern land. *Austromancy* combines the Latin south wind and the Greek word for divination; it means foretelling the future from observation of the winds. The chief of our Weather Bureau is an *austromancer*.

Austria is not derived from the same root, but from German *Österreich*, eastern kingdom.

awkward

Probably from Old Norse *afug*, turned the wrong way, back foremost, combined with the suffix -*ward*, in the direction of; i.e., in an *awk* direction. Why do we never use *awk* without its suffix? An *awk* stroke in tennis would be backhanded. In Sir Thomas Malory's *Le Morte d'Arthur* we find: "With an awke stroke gave him a grete wounde."

In old writings we also find *awkly*, *awkness*; and *awky*, meaning difficult.

bashful

A *bashful* girl is shy and self-consciously modest, full of *bash;* though no one seems to use *bash* as a noun nowadays. Bosley Crowther, in a review in the New York *Times,* March 1950, spoke of an actress behaving "boldly and bashlessly," or without *bash. Bash,* an aphetic form of *abash,* comes to us via French from the Latin *baire,* to astound, regarded as formed on *bah!,* a natural expression of amazement in any language. It is what you utter when your jaw drops open. (See *abeyance.*) To *abash* someone is to destroy his self-possession so that he gapes with surprise. Roger Ascham, Queen Elizabeth's tutor, wrote: "If a yong jentleman . . . be bashefull, and will soon blushe, they call him a babishe and ill brought up thyng."

The verb *bash,* as in "bash his brains out," has nothing to do with blushes, but comes probably from a Scandinavian root related to Swedish *basa,* to flog or beat. Or it may be an onomatopœic word, combining the "b" of beat and bang with dash and lash.

Abase is not a related word, though a doughty *bash* will lay you low, but comes from the Latin *basus,* of short or low stature.

bawdy

The derivation is unknown, but Skeat suggests Welsh *bawaidd*, dirty, from *baw*, mud. Other sources suggest a relationship to Old French *baud, baude,* bold, lively, gay, merry, which sense has passed into our *wanton,* who is a lady both slightly muddy and highly gay. Langland in *Piers Plowman,* in 1362, uses a good word—*Bawdstrot*—meaning bold strut.

bead

Old English *biddan*, to pray. The name was transferred from the prayer to the small spheres used for "telling beads," a sort of strung abacus for counting the number of prayers said. We now have so far forgotten the religious origin that we have *beads* in a necklace, *beads* of sweat on a brow or nose, *beads* on a frosted glass of beer; and the act of drawing a *bead*—looking through a gunsight at the target.

bedridden

Old English *bedridan*, to ride a bed. The unfortunate who can no longer sit a horse has to ride his bed. *Bed* is probably from Aryan *bhodh*, to dig, as if originally a *bed* was a dug-out place, a lair. A *garden-bed* fits in with this root idea perfectly (no pun intended).

beguile

Old English *bigile*, to cheat thoroughly, probably a word of Teutonic origin, meaning to delude, deceive, cheat; cognate with *wile*. The word has entirely lost its sinister connotation and has come to mean to charm, to divert, to amuse.

Amuse went through a similar metamorphosis. It is from Old French *amuser*, to put into a stupid stare, to cause to muse, to divert the attention from the facts, to delude, to cheat. This definition still applies, in a way, to *amusement* as escapism. The average movie-goer is diverted from the facts.

belfry

This word for a bell-tower has nothing to do with bells, except by association. Originally, a *belfry* was a movable tower used by besiegers, rolled up close to the walls of the attacked city. Later, it was a tower to protect watchmen, a watch-tower in which alarm bells were hung; hence, finally, a bell-tower.

The root is German *bergfrid*, Old High German *fridu* place, security, place of shelter, and *bergen*, to protect, defend.

In Italian *belfry* is *battifredo*, assimilated by popular etymology with *battere* to beat, to strike (as a clock).

bewilder

This Old English word meant to lead one astray; literally, to lose in pathless places, in a wilderness. When we are "bewitched, bothered and bewildered," we are figuratively lost in the wilderness. *Wilderness* was, in early Britain, wild land where the deer roamed, from the Old English *wilde'or*, wild deer.

A *wild goose chase* was at first a kind of horse-race in which the second or any succeeding horse had to follow accurately the course of the leader, at a definite interval, like the orderly flight of wild geese in the autumn sky. In Nicholas Breton's *Mother's Blessing*, 1602, we find: "Esteem a horse, according to his pace, But loose no wagers on a wilde goose chase."

In later use, the horses were forgotten, and such a pursuit referred to something as unlikely to be caught as the fast-flying wild goose. From *Romeo and Juliet*: "Nay, if thy wits run the wild-goose chase, I have done; for thou hast more of the wild-goose in one of thy wits than, I am sure, I have in my whole five."

blue peter

The blue flag with a white square in its center, hoisted by a ship as the signal of immediate sailing, is called the *blue peter*. The "blue" part is obvious; but why "peter"? By some authorities this is said to be a corruption of French *partir*, leave or notice of departure. According to Falconer, it is rather a corruption of "repeater."

The purpose of the flag is twofold: to call all sailors aboard, and to give notice to the port that any person having money-claims may make them before the ship pulls out. Or else!

blue-stocking

A term no girl, however intellectual, likes to have applied to her, as it connotes a certain precious and unalluring pedantry. The term is found as early as the 17th century, applied to the "Little Parliament" of 1653, ridiculing the puritanically plain dress of the members (all men, of course).

The present sense of *blue-stocking* originated in connection with reunions, held in London about 1750, at the houses of Mrs. Montague, Mrs. Vesey, and Mrs. Ord, three intellectual ladies who considered that card-playing was not the only way to pass an evening. They gave parties where conversations on literary subjects or other intellectual matters were earnestly nurtured, and they invited eminent men of letters. These 18th-century radicals rebelled against "full dress," and one daring gentleman, Mr. Benjamin Stillingfleet, always wore blue worsted instead of black silk stockings. Admiral Boscawen is said to have derisively dubbed the coterie "the Blue Stocking Society."

bomb

This nightmare of our century, whether A or H, had an innocuous origin in French *bombe,* Spanish *bomba,* probably from *bombo,* a bumming or humming noise, such as a *bumble-bee* makes. We get *boom* direct from the Latin *bombus. Bombus* is a doctor's term for a humming in the ears or a growling in the stomach, that embarrassing signal of emptiness. A *bombardier beetle* is a genus that, when irritated, ejects fluid with a sharp report and blue vapor.

bonanza

This U.S. colloquialism, a Spanish word, meaning fair weather, prosperity, from Latin *bonus,* good, was originally a miner's expression for good luck, for unearthing a body of rich ore. It was first so used in 1866, of the silver mines on the Comstock lode.

Bonus, from Latin *good* (*man*), when used to mean a good thing should, grammatically, be *bonum.* Our present use—a boon or gift over and above what is normally due, something to the good—probably originated as stock-exchange slang. I believe these Latinists hailed from London, not from Wall Street.

In 1773, Macklin, in *The Man of the World,* wrote: "Got my share of the clothing . . . the contracts, the lottery tickets, and aw the political bonuses."

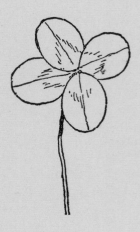

bonfire

From *bone fire*, a fire of bones. We usually think of a bonfire as the brightest outdoor part in some celebration such as the Fourth of July; but its origin was less lively. In the Middle Ages, a *bone-fire* (it was so spelled till 1760) was a funeral pyre for burning the bodies of plague victims; a fire for burning witches, heretics, proscribed books. Johnson, in 1755 in his *Dictionary*, decided the word was "bonfire" and derived it "from, *bon*, good (French) and fire." The original charnel meaning was forgotten.

boot-legger

Our hero and provider of Prohibition days, one who carries liquor in his tall boot-legs. As early as 1890, this picturesque word was used in the *New York Voice*: "The 'bootlegger' is a grim spectre to the anti-Prohibitionist. . . . He is a man who wears boots in whose tops are concealed a flask or two of liquor."

By transference, we now speak of other *boot-legged* commodities—the sale of banned books in Boston, the smuggling of Mexicans across the Texas border, the dissemination of ideas behind the Iron Curtain.

bric-a-brac

This word for artistic curiosities, knick-knacks, antique odds and ends such as our grandmothers used to keep in the corner whatnot to enchant visiting children, is French and is said to be formed after the phrase *de bric et de broc*, by hook or by crook. Thackeray, in his *Paris Sketch Book*, noted that "The Palace of Versailles has been turned into a bricabrac shop. Mark Twain, in *A Tramp Abroad*, described himself as a "bric-a-bracker," because of the odds and ends he picked up.

Knick-knack, a reduplication of *knack*, a rap, originally meant a petty trick or subterfuge. How the word came to mean a pleasing trifle, a trinket, is not clear, though the French *tours de main*, a turn of the hand, as in conjuring, is translated as *knack*, and possibly the small articles used in sleight-of-hand were called *knick-knacks*. To "have the knack" means to possess the know-how.

brown

This name of a color comes to us through the Teutonic, but can be traced back to the Aryan root, *bhru*, a beaver, because of the color of his silky woman-prized pelt. The early sense of the word in English was dusky or dark, we gather from Dr. Johnson's *Dictionary*, or from such early authors as Maundeville (*c.* 1400), who says: "Here colour is liche Vyolet, or more browne than the Violettes."

Related words, through the Latin *brunus*, are *brunette*, French for "a nut-browne girl"; *burn*, a process of browning; and *burnish*. To muse, to fall into "a brown study" is an old expression, found as long ago as 1532.

brunt

A short, harsh word, sounding indeed like something difficult to bear, its origin is unsure, but perhaps it was Old Norse *bruna*, to advance with the speed of fire. It is possible that there was some association with "burnt" (in Scotland "brunt") as if the "chief brunt" were "the hottest part of the battle."

bugbear

This object of dread, usually of needless and imaginary terror, has nothing at all to do with bugs. It is derived from Middle English *bugge*, possibly from Welsh *bwg*, a ghost, hobgoblin, scarecrow; and was thought to be a hobgoblin in the shape of a bear which ate up naughty children.

bugger

From Latin *Bulgaris*, Bulgarian, a name given to a sect of heretics who came from Bulgaria in the 11th century. Afterwards, the epithet was applied to other heretics to whom abominable practices were ascribed; hence, it came to be a synonym for sodomites. The Oxford *New English Dictionary* primly says: "In decent use only as a legal term," but admits that in English dialect and in the U.S., bugger often means merely chap, fellow, with no insult implied as to perversion.

bulldozer

That huge prehistoric monster of a machine which you see pushing earth and rocks around a building site got its name from U.S. slang; to *bull-dose* was to administer a severe dose of flogging. It was first applied, in a newspaper of 1876, to vigilantes who beat up Negroes trying to vote in Louisiana.

A large pistol, calculated to bully or intimidate, was called a *bull-dozer*, too.

buxom

Early Middle English *buhsum*, from the stem of *bow*, with the suffix *-some*, meaning easily bowed or bent, obedient, pliable, tractable. This word has undergone a complete change in meaning since its early life. J. Bell, in 1581, used it thus: "The Consuls should . . . sweare faythfully to become bonnaire and buxome to the Pope."

Now, *buxom* is used to describe a woman who is full of healthful vigor, plump and comely, comfortable-looking, and not necessarily pliant at all. *Buxom* is generally a polite euphemism for stout, and no woman wants to be it.

Except in the mind's picture of a *buxom* woman, well-rounded, the word is not connected with *bosom*, which is perhaps from Old Aryan arm or bough. Like the partially synonymous *fathom*, *bosom* originally meant the space embraced by the two arms, as in "Come to my bosom" or "in Abraham's bosom." A *bosom friend* is the closest one to you. In the South, Negro stevedores on Mississippi steamers carry large, flat loaves of bread in their shirt-fronts for quick snacks on the job. They call them *bosom-bread*.

Bough is from Aryan *bhagus*, arm or leg. The *bow* of a ship is ultimately the same word, but enters English via Scandinavian or Low German.

Bonnaire (see quotation above) is short for *debonnaire* (of good mien), and a pleasant word that we ought to revive. *Fathom* comes from Old English *fæðm*, the two arms outstretched, or, roughly measured, six feet. The original meaning included the idea of embrace, bosom, and the object of embrace, as in "the wife of thy bosom." Figuratively, as a verb, *fathom* means breadth of comprehension. The idea of depth, of nautical soundings, came later. A *fathometer* is a gadget on shipboard for measuring depth.

by and large

This phrase, which we use *by and large* to mean "on the whole," over-all, in general, is a nautical term, and to a sailor it means to turn the ship to the wind, within six points, just as *full and by* also means sailing close-hauled to the wind. Captain Smith in *Seaman's Grammar*, 1627, wrote: "Fill the Sails, keep full, full and by"; and Sturmy, in *The Mariner's Magazine* of 1669, said: "Thus you see the ship handled in fair weather and foul, by and large."

caboodle

U.S. slang, a corruption of *kit and boodle*. The "whole caboodle" means the whole lot (of persons or things). The component parts came to us thus: *kit*, from Middle Dutch *kitte*, a wooden tankard with hooped staves; a container or box, a basket; a collection of articles (articles of *kit*) forming part of a soldier's equipment. Also, the knapsack itself that held the *kit*. *Boodle* is historically obscure, but it may be Dutch *boedel*, meaning estate, possession, stock.

calendar

Latin *calendarium*, account-book, from *kalendæ*, days on which accounts were due, usually the first of the month. The Roman housewife had her troubles, too. The days of the week, as we know them, are a mixture of Roman and Norse myth: *Sunday*, worship of the sun; *Monday*, the moon's day; *Tuesday*, Tiw's day, Teutonic god of war; *Wednesday*, Woden's day (hence the irrational "d"); *Thursday*, day of Thor, god of thunder; *Friday*, named for Frigga, wife of Woden; *Saturday* for Saturn of the Romans.

The months got their names this way:

January: from Latin *janua*, door or gate. Janus was the god of doors and gates, hence of all beginnings. A door has two sides, Janus two faces, looking forward and back. A *janitor* watches the door.

February: Latin *Februa*, feast of expiation, cleansing.

March: Latin *Mars*, god of war. The French name for Tuesday— *Mardi*—honors him too.

April: Latin *aprire*, to open. Spring is the time when buds, leaves, hearts, open. An *apéritif* opens the meal or the digestive tract.

May: Latin, goddess Maia.

June: Roman family Junius.

July: This month, so called to honor Julius Cæsar, was formerly *Quintilius*, the fifth. The first Roman month was March.

August: for Augustus Cæsar.

September: 7th month.

October: 8th month.

November: 9th month.

December: 10th month.

camera

Latin *camera*, vault, arched chamber, probably from the Aryan root *kam*, to curve or bend. This word, until popularized by the advent of photography, was used as an architectural term only, as in the phrase "in camera," in the judge's chambers, or in *bicameral*, of a two-house legislature. *Camera obscura* is a dark chamber; *camera lucida* a light one. As a photographic term, *camera* was first used by Daguerre, the French inventor of the *daguerrotype*, around 1850.

Kodak, now loosely used as a generic name for any camera, rightly belongs only to the Eastman product. The word was invented, an arbitrary but successful combination of letters, by Mr. George Eastman for trade-mark purposes. He created his Kodak in 1888.

cataract

The Latin *cataracta*, waterfall, floodgate, came from Greek *katarasso*, rush down, down-rushing, as water or a swooping eagle; to dash headlong, as rain or a river. The earliest English use is found in *Genesis*, where *cataracts* were the flood-gates of heaven, keeping back the rain.

The pathological use, opacity of the lens of the eye, is figurative: a *cataract* obstructs the vision as a portcullis does a gateway, a flood-gate a stream.

From the Greek root *kata-*, down, we also get *cataclysm*, to wash down, dash, as a wave, a deluge; a political or social upheaval that sweeps away the old order. *Catalogue* is from pick or choose down, reckon up, a list from which you make your choice, as in Sears, Roebuck or Montgomery Ward. *Catapult* is a machine for hurling down stones. *Catarrh* is a flowing down, as any one with a head cold well knows. *Catastrophe* is a turning down, an overturn. *Catawampous* is a made-up U.S. slang term meaning fierce, unsparing, destructive. *Category* is from the Greek *kategoria*, an assembly, a public speaking place, an accusation, to speak against. Aristotle talked of his ten *categories*, the meaning of which has fired philosophers from then to now.

His ten *categories* or predicaments or classifications were: (1) Substance or Being, (2) Quantity, (3) Quality, (4) Relation, (5) Place, (6) Time, (7) Posture, (8) Having or Possession, (9) Action, (10) Passion. Which seems to cover everything except humor. The word *category* long ago lost the sense of public accusation, and now means merely a class to which a certain assertion applies, or a class in any general scheme of classification; and *categorical* has taken on the sense of absolute, unqualified.

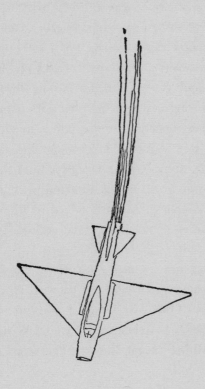

catholic

This comes from the Greek *katholicos,* meaning entirely, whole; general, universal. We retain the original meaning in the phrases "of catholic taste," "a catholic point of view." The ecclesiastical use may be found in Smith's *Dictionary of Christian Antiquity,* where it is explained that the name "the catholic church" or "church universal" was first applied to the whole body of believers as distinguished from an individual congregation.

After the separation of East and West, *Catholic* was assumed as its descriptive epithet by the Western or Latin church, as *Orthodox* was by the Eastern or Greek. *Orthodox* is Greek, meaning right in opinion. Following the Reformation, the terms Anglo-Catholic and Roman Catholic came into use.

An author of 1551, T. Wilson, in *Logike* said: "Catholike being a greeke word signifieth nothing in English but universall or common"; and Dekker, in 1607 in *Northward Hoe,* wrote: "What is more catholick i' the city than for husbands daily for to forgive the nightly sins of their bedfellows?" Here "catholick" means not only common and universal, but broad-minded.

chum

This school-boyish term of intimacy is conjectured to be a familiar abbreviation of chamber-fellow, chamber-mate. Its first recorded use was in 1684 when Creech dedicated his *Theocritus* to "my chum Mr. Hody of Wadham College."

Chummage means the quartering of two or more in the same room.

In Maine, bait broadcast on the sea to attract fish is called *chum*. Perhaps this is derived from *chump* or *champ* —to gnaw or nibble.

cliché

French *cliquer*, to click, applied in France to the sound
made in the striking of melted lead in order to obtain a
proof or cast; a printer's term for a stereotype block; hence,
stereotyped speech such as Frank Sullivan lampoons in
The New Yorker.

Lampoon is from French *lamponner*, to ridicule, from
lampons, let us drink, and *lamper*, a slang word for booze
or guzzle. *Lampas* is a disease horses get, producing in-
tense thirst.

cloth or material

Most materials get their names from the place where they were originally made, though a few are amusingly descriptive—*chenille*, that softly furry stuff, is the French word for caterpillar, which grew out of Latin *canicula*, little dog. *Cambric* and *chambray* are both from Kameryk, the Flemish name of Cambray; *calico* is from Calicut on the coast of Malabar; *cashmere* from the Vale of Kashmir where the Tibetan goats grow the finest white wool shawls on their backs. *Cheviot* is made of wool from the sheep in the Cheviot Hills of England; *cretonne* comes from Creton in Normandy; *corduroy* was, in French, *corde du roi*, King's cloth, though some authorities prefer to derive it from *cœur du roi*, King's heart. Stiff *crinoline* is from two Latin words, *crinus*, horse-hair, and *linum*, flax thread. *Damask* came from Damascus, also famous for *damascene* steel and swords. *Denim*, that blue-jean uniform of American youth and workman, was cloth *de Nîmes* (of the city of Nîmes), and *jeans* is an English way of saying Genoa. *Duffel* (as in duffel bag) came from Duffel near Antwerp; *dimity* is from Latin *dimitos*, two threads. Rough *frieze* came from Friesland; *gingham* was a Malay word for striped; *georgette* was named for a French dressmaker of the 19th century, Mme Georgette de la Plante; *gauze* came from Biblical Gaza; *gabardine* was Old French for pilgrim's cloak; *khaki* from the Hindu word for dusty; *lawn* from Laon in France; *lisle* from Lille; *madras* was from the city of Madras in India; *melton* from Melton

Mowbray, a great hunting-place in Leicestershire, in England; *muslin* from Italian *mussolina*, diminutive of Mosul in Mesopotamia. (Il Duce's progenital home?)

Nainsook is from a charming Sanskrit word meaning "delight of the eye"; *poplin* from French *popeline*, because the cloth was made at Avignon, once the seat of the Pope. *Pongee* was from the Chinese words denoting cloth made on a family's own loom; *taffeta* from Persian *taftan*, to twist or spin; *seersucker*, that striped summer boon to men, from Persian "milk and sugar." *Velvet* is from French *velu*, shaggy, as is *velours*; and *voile* is the French word for sail, from Latin *velum*, sail, curtain, or covering. To *reveal* is to pull the curtain back.

conspiracy

When spies and plotters are convicted of *conspiracy*, they have literally been putting their heads close as in harmonizing and *breathing* together, as this word is from Latin *conspirare*, to breathe together. Other words from this root are *inspire*, to breathe in, the breath of the god perhaps; *respiration*, breathing again and again; *perspire*, to breathe through your pores; *aspire*, to breathe toward, hopefully.

coof

On Nantucket Island this gently contemptuous term is used to designate an "off-islander," a summer visitor. I have met *coof* nowhere else in the United States, but, according to the *Oxford Dictionary*, the word is current in Scotland and means a dull, spiritless fellow; one somewhat obtuse in sense and sensibility. O Nantucketers, for shame! Perhaps *coof* is identified with the English "cove," slang for fellow. Burns used it in *For A' That*: "Tho' hundreds worship at his word, He's but a coof for a' that."

cordon bleu

In France, the knights of the ancient order of the St. Esprit (the Holy Ghost) wore a decoration suspended on a blue ribbon, a "cordon bleu." The commander, de Souvé, Comte d'Olonne, and his fellows met at a sort of club, which was noted for the choiceness of its food. Hence, when anyone dined exceptionally well, he said: *"C'est un vrai repas de cordon bleu,"* which came to be a synonym for superfine cookery. The *Cordon Bleu* cooking school in Paris has long turned out artists of the stove; and now there is one in New York, run by Dione Lucas, famous for her omelets on East 52nd Street.

couple

From Latin *copula*, bond, band, tie, connection. Originally, this was the leather bond that tied two hounds together to hunt in *couples*, in leash. To *copulate* is to fasten together, to link, to couple, not necessarily for sexual ends.

When we talk of a *brace* of dogs, or of partridges (two birds being the right number for a meal), we mean a couple, though in the original sense the *brace* was the leash or binding, from Latin *brachia*, two arms, a fathom (see *embrace*). In the nautical sense, to "brace a yard" means to fasten or tighten it.

crazy

From Old French *acraser*, derived from Norse. The Swedish word *krasa* means to crackle, and *slå i kras* to dash in pieces. Just what happens to your mind when you go crazy. Originally, *to craze* meant to break or crush objects—a shield, a pitcher, tin ore in a mine, crackle-ware in pottery, with its "crazed" glaze. A *crazy-quilt* is patchwork, small irregular bits sewn together. Zoologists say there is no basis in natural history for the expression "Crazy like a fox," unless it is ironic, Reynard being notoriously clever. *Crash* is from the same root.

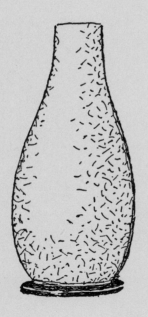

cream

From Latin *chrisma*, derived from the Greek word for unction, anointing. *Christ* is the Anointed. Originally, *cream* was the mixture of oil and balm used in administering certain church sacraments. The goo women put on their faces at night, *cold cream*—what, by the way, is hot cream?—is still composed of oil and balm. The *cream* in your coffee is something different.

dark horse

This is, of course, a racing term for a promising horse of which nothing is positively known by the general public, and whose speed and performance are kept dark from betters and bookmakers. Figuratively, in politics, a *dark horse* is a surprise candidate entered in the race at the last minute and expected to astound the voters by his speed. A British newspaper paragraph of 1886 first used the expression: "At last a Liberal candidate has entered the field at Croydon. The Conservatives have kept their candidate back, as a dark horse."

In 1946, I saw a white *dark horse*, Airborne, a great plodding cart-puller he looked, win the Derby at fine odds. My daughter bet on him for no better reason than that she had known a paratrooper during the war.

deserts

A derivative of *deserve*, this word with the accent on the second syllable comes via Old French *deservir* from Latin *deservire*, meaning to serve zealously, well, or meritoriously; later, to merit by service, as in the phrase "get your just deserts." Your *deserts* may be either reward or punishment, according to your deeds or misdeeds, and they are almost always plural.

To *desert*, abandon, is from an entirely different Latin word, *deserere*, to sever connection with someone or something. *Desert* (accent on the first syllable), as in sandy Africa or Arizona, is from Latin *desertus*, abandoned, left waste.

Dessert, the sweets or fruits you eat after the serious part of dinner, is from Latin via the French word *desservir*, to take away what has been served, to clear the table. Mr. Pepys, in his *Diary* for July 12, 1666, wrote: "The dessert coming, with roses upon it, The Duchesse bid him try."

desultory

Latin *desultor*, one who leaps down, a vaulter, a circus-horse-leaper. When you engage in *desultory* conversation you are jumping from one horse to another, very often in midstream. Your talk is random, disconnected, skipping about.

If you *insult* someone, you leap on him—usually figuratively, but not always. If two people *consult*, they jump together. *Results* are consequences that leap back at you.

detergent

This is a new word in the housewife's vocabulary for magic dirt-chasers, but really an old one, as we find it in a publication of 1616 called *Country Farms*. It is from Latin *detergere*, to wipe away. It is not related to *deter*, which is from Latin *deterrere*, to frighten away; though a good *detergent* does frighten away the grease on your pots and pans.

dime

That thin silver ten-cent piece of U.S. currency was originally the *tithe* (tenth) paid by unwilling taxees to the church or to a temporal ruler. We find the word as "dymes" in Langland's *Piers Plowman,* written in 1362. Its origin is via Old French *disme* from Latin *decima,* tithe, tenth part. The U.S. coin dates from 1786.

Dime novel was used by Henry George in 1879: "The boy who reads dime novels wants to be a pirate."

Related words are *decimal,* tenth part, and *decimate,* to cut off every tenth head. See also *December* under *calendar.*

disheveled

This word comes through Old French *deschevelé*, meaning the hair is out of bounds, from medieval Latin *discapillatus*, stripped of hair, shaven. A *disheveled* woman was one without her coif or headdress, hence, with hair unconfined and flung about in disorder. The word has come to mean generally untidy, in dishabille. When a girl is fresh from the beauty parlor, her hair in smooth curls, why don't we say she is *sheveled*?

dismal

First mentioned in 1256 as the English or Anglo-French name for French *les mals jours*, the evil days, whence it appears to be Old French *dis mal*, from Latin *dies mali*, evil or unlucky days. *Dismal* was thus originally a substantive of collective meaning; when "days" was added (as in "summer days," "winter days"), its attributive use passed into an adjective, and, its primary application obscured, it was finally, before 1600, extended from *day* to be a general attribute of anything gloomy, dejected, somber, dreary, depressing.

The *dies mali* were the unpropitious days of the medieval calendar, when it was unwise to begin any undertaking. Also called *dies Ægyptiaci*, Egyptian days, because they were first computed by Egyptian astrologers. Chaucer connected them with the plagues of Biblical Egypt, and treats the word as if it is Old French *dis mal*, ten evils, or plagues. He wrote in *Dethe Blaunche*: "I trove hyt was in the dismalle, That was the X woundes of Egipte."

The *dies mali* were January 1 and 25, February 4 and 26, March 1 and 28, April 10 and 20—and so on through the year, two per month.

The U.S. Weather Bureau in New York City, in February, 1950, startled New Yorkers by forecasting a "dismal" day; a prediction that brought forth the following delectable paragraph by E. B. White in the "Notes and Comment" department of *The New Yorker* for February 25, 1950:*

The most startling news in the paper on February 13th was the weather forecast. It was "Rainy and dismal." When we read the word "dismal" in the *Times*, we knew that the era of pure science was drawing to a close and the day of philosophical science was at hand. (Probably in the nick of time.) Consider what had happened! A meteorologist, whose job was simply to examine the instruments in his observatory, had done a quick switch and had examined the entrails of birds. In his fumbling way he had attempted to predict the impact of the elements on the human spirit. His was a poor attempt, as it turned out, but it was an attempt. There are, of course, no evil days in nature, no *dies mali*, and the forecast plainly showed that the weatherman had been spending his time indoors. To the intimates of rain, no day is dismal, and a dull sky is as plausible as any other. Nevertheless, the forecast indicated that the connection had been reestablished between nature and scientific man. Now, all we need is a meteorologist who has once been soaked to the skin without ill effect. No one can write knowingly of weather who walks bent over on wet days.

Dixie

Just why the Southern tier of states is called by this rollicking collective name is obscure, but the most plausible explanation I have found is tied up with money issued by a New Orleans bank, before the Civil War. On the back of each ten-dollar bill, for the benefit of the French-speaking citizens, was printed the French word for ten, *Dix*; hence Louisiana, and eventually the rest of the South, became known as the land of *Dixies—Dixieland*. It was about this time that Daniel Emmet, Negro minstrel and songwriter, homesick for Southern warmth in chill New York, composed *Away Down South in Dixie*. The infectious tune popularized the name.

The Mason and Dixon Line, that imaginary boundary between Maryland and Pennsylvania separating "free" from "slave" states, is not related etymologically to Dixie. Charles Mason and Jeremiah Dixon were two English astronomers who made a survey between the years 1763–7 to end a territorial dispute between the Baltimores and the Penns. The use of the *M. and D. Line* as delineating free from slave states dates from debates in Congress over the Missouri Compromise, 1819–20.

dragoon

An early kind of carbine or musket was a *dragoon* because it breathed fire like the fabulous dragon. What would those early military fellows have called a flame-thrower? Later, the cavalry soldier who wielded the *dragoon musket* became, himself, a *dragoon*. As a verb, the word means to force or drive, to persecute. The etymology of *dragon* is, obscurely, from the Greek stem "to see clearly." Possibly reluctant *dragons*, or eager ones, had good vision.

dreary

From Old English *dréorig*, gory, bloody, sorrowful, sad. Spenser, in *The Faerie Queene* (1590), used the word in its more grim sense: "With their drery wounds, and bloody gore." Time has alleviated *dreary* to mean merely full of melancholy, doleful, dismal, repulsively dull or uninteresting. A *dreary* party is bloody only in the English slang sense.

ebullience

This word comes from Latin *ebullire*, to boil over. An *ebullient* fellow is a man who bubbles over with extravagant enthusiasm, like boiling water. There is an instrument for ascertaining the strength of distilled liquors by observing the boiling point which is called an *ebullioscope*. Unfortunately, it is not adapted to determine the boiling point of men and nations, which might be a good safety-valve at times. Russia would then know when to stop shoving people around.

elegant

This word is related to the Latin *eligere*, to select. The etymological sense of choosing carefully or skillfully survives in "elegant dress." In early Latin *elegans* was a term of reproach, used of a dainty, foppish male, but by classical times it expressed notions of refined luxury and grace. The slang use—as in "elegant butter," "elegant roast beef"—began about 1848.

embarrass

From Latin *inbarre,* to bar, literally to block, obstruct, as with a *barrier. Barricade* is not from the same root but from Spanish *barrica,* a cask, the first street *barricades* in Paris being composed of casks filled with earth, paving-stones, or other heavy matter.

enclave

This term, used after World War II to describe the U.S. zone in Berlin, for example, comes from Late Latin *inclavare*, meaning to lock in. *Clavis* is key. A bit of territory entirely surrounded by foreign dominions is thus locked in with a key. In carpentry, an *enclave* is a dovetail, keyed in. From the same root: *clef*, the key in music, *clavichord*, key strings, *clavicle*, small key or bolt, from the shape of the collarbone, *klavier*, the German name for piano.

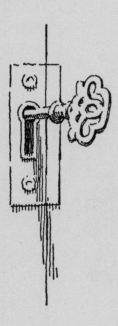

enormous

From Latin *enorma*, out of line with a mason's square or pattern, this word first meant deviating from the ordinary rule or type, unusual, extraordinary, extravagant; only later did it take on the sense of large, vast, monstrous. *Abnormal* is also away from the mason's square or usual pattern. If you name your daughter *Norma* you expect her to grow up according to pattern, a model girl, not a genius.

eschew

A word of Teutonic origin, Old English *scéoh*, shy, from a Teutonic root *skeuhw*, to fear, to terrify. The shy person fears situations and people, and *eschews* them. When a horse *shies* skittishly, something along the bridle path has frightened him. To be *shy of* something, lacking, is betting slang. A *shyster*, a U.S. slang term for a shady or disreputable lawyer, may be from this race-track form of shy. When we find in *Blackwell's Magazine* the sentence "Gambling hells and shy saloons," the author certainly didn't mean timid.

esoteric

This word, from Greek *esoterikos,* inner, was used to describe the secret doctrines taught by Pythagoras to a select few among his disciples. Hence the word means, in reference to philosophic doctrines: designed for an inner circle of advanced or privileged disciples; of motives: not openly avowed. The antonym is *exoteric,* outside, external, used of philosophic ideas designed for the generality of disciples; intelligible to the public, therefore simple and commonplace. *Exotic* means foreign, alien, introduced from abroad, not indigenous. Orchids are *exotic* to the United States, as are Communism, sarongs, and Afghan hounds.

etch

Old Teutonic *atjan*, causative of *etan* to eat; to cause to eat or to be eaten. When the artist *etches* metal or stone, he eats away the surface with acids. Have you *etched* your lunch yet? The time-worn innuendo, that invitation from gentleman to lady—"Come up and see my etchings sometime"—now, under the etymological microscope, turns into a respectable invitation to tea or dinner.

exorbitant

From Late Latin *exorbita*, out of the wheel-track. An *ex-orbitant* price is one beyond the normal expectation of the shopper; *exorbitant* ideas deviate from the rule, often flagrantly. The current poetic slang phrase for something wonderful beyond measure—"out of this world"—describes a girl, a boy, a spring hat, which is outside the everyday wheel-track of experience.

Orb, a sphere, the world, is from Latin *orbis*, ring or circle, round disk. In astronomy, the orb of a planet or star is that space on the celestial sphere within which its pull is supposed to act. Also, *orb* is poet's talk for eye. *Orbit* is the path or wheel-track of a heavenly body, or of an influential person.

expedite

From Latin *expedem,* meaning from the foot. Literally, when you *expedite* a piece of business, you free a person's feet from fetters, leaving him clear to move forward—"footloose and fancy free." Related words are *expeditious, expediency. Impede* is the opposite—to put fetters on the foot, or a stumbling block in front of it. *Impedimenta*—baggage—hinders you when you travel. To *impeach* someone in high office is, by roundabout etymology, from the same root: Middle English *enpechen, empesche,* Old French *empechier,* Late Latin *impedicare,* to catch, entangle, from *pedicare,* fetter, from *pes, pedem* foot.

fan

This jocular abbreviation of *fanatic* (from Latin *fanum*, temple, or one who worships) used in expressions such as "Sinatra fan," "Ranger fan," "fan mail," is scarcely modern slang, since it appeared as early as 1682 in *New News from Bedlam*: "The Loyal Phans to abuse." Sounds like Ebbets Field.

To *fan* at a ball, or an electric *fan*, is from Old English *fann*, from Latin *vannus*, a basket used to winnow grain. Weather-*vane* is from the same root.

feckless

Here is another of those words which we use only in the negative. Why is no one ever *feckful* when he is vigorous and efficient? Why isn't the purport, drift or substance of a statement its *feck*? *Feck* is Scottish dialect for *effect*, or hardy and vigorous. An early quotation, *circa* 1500, says: "This is the fek of our entent."

fiasco

This is the Italian word for flask or bottle. How this came to mean a breakdown or failure in a performance, how "far fiasco," to make a bottle, achieved its figurative use, is obscure, but Italian etymologists have proposed various guesses. The most plausible relates to the Venetian blowers of fine glass, who, when the glass showed a flaw, spoiling it for goblets or bowls, set it aside to make common bottles. The word *flask* is found in nearly all Romance and Teutonic languages, in closely related forms.

fifth column

First used of the collaborators and quislings (which see—
a term not yet minted then) in the Spanish Civil War,
1936–9. "Secret sympathizers and subverters," the *fifth
column*, "the Franco sympathizers within Madrid . . .
(were) so described in a radio address by General Mola
when he was leading four columns of troops against the
city" (Webster). J. Alvarez del Vayo, in his *Freedom's
Battle*, 1942, used the term.

flamingo

These birds decorated with flame-colored feathers were first mentioned in Hakluyt's *Voyages* in 1565. The word is from Spanish *flamenco*, from Roman *flama*, flame. From the same root comes the ardent Spanish dance, the *flamenco*; *inflammable*, capable of burning; *flagrant*, used to describe an offense so serious it is blazing; and *flamboyant*, which reaches English via French *flambe*, flame. A *flamboyant* costume is flamingly colored. In architecture, *flamboyancy* connotes waved lines in flame-like forms. I remember seeing *flamboyant* trees in the Virgin Islands, brilliant with flame-colored flowers.

flower

This word comes to us via the Latin *florem*, *flos*, from the Aryan root *bhlo-*, to blow. *Blow* means to blossom or bloom. *Flourish* is a doublet of *flower*. *Deflower* is to take off the bloom, as of virgins.

Flour, as in baking, is from French *fleur de faine*, the flower of the finest part of the ground meal. In Dr. Johnson's *Dictionary*, 1755, there is no distinction between *flower* and *flour*.

Many flowers were named after some noted botanist or scientist: *fuchsia* for the German Fuchs; *wistaria* (sometimes spelled wisteria) for Wistar, an American anatomist; *gardenias* for Dr. Alexander Garden, vice president of the Royal Society of Botanists. *Sage*, which was early used as a medicine, is from Latin *salvus*, saved. *Peony* is from *Paion*, healer of the gods in Greek mythology; *centauria* from Chiron the centaur; *dianthus* from the two Greek words, *dios*, god, Zeus, and *anthos*, flower.

Aster describes itself—a star—in Latin. *Calendula* bloomed at the calends (see *calendar*). *Campanula* is little bell; *chrysanthemum*, gold flower; *daisy* is Anglo-Saxon *dæges-eage*, the day's eye; *dandelion*, whose petals are toothed, if you look carefully, is French *dent de lion*, lion's tooth. *Digitalis*, foxglove, early known as a heart stimulant, is from Latin *digit*, finger, I suppose because your finger just fits into a deep-throated bell. An Irish friend of mine calls them "fairy thimbles." *Geranium* means, in Latin, crane's bill, and that is what the seed resembles.

Gladiolus is little sword, as wielded by the Roman *gladi-
ator. Helianthus* is Greek sunflower; *heliotrope,* turning to
the sun. *Iris* is the Roman goddess of the rainbow. *Phlox*
is Greek for flame. *Nasturtium* is Latin for nose-torment-
ing, so named, according to Pliny, for its pungent, acrid
smell. *Pansy,* with its thoughtful velvet face, is from
French *pensée,* thought. *Camellia,* new religion of the
South, was named by Linnæus after Kamel (Latinized
Camellus), a Moravian Jesuit who first described the
flora of the Island of Luzon. *Poinsettia,* a species of eu-
phorbia native to Mexico, and now ineluctably part of
Christmas along with the more northerly Santa Claus and
snow, was named in 1836 for J. R. Poinsett, American
Minister to Mexico, who first "discovered" the scarlet fo-
liage. No doubt the Mexicans had noticed it before.

fond

This is from Middle English *fonned*, where it originally meant that which has lost its flavor, insipid, sickly-flavored. About 1830 Wyclif wrote: "zif þe salt be fonnyd it is not worþi." *Fond* traveled through five changes of sense before, in Shakespeare's time, it grew to be, like a Henry Green title, loving. Lyly in *Euphues*, 1580, has: "He yat is young thinketh the olde man fond"—infatuated, foolish, silly. From there, the word became synonymous with idiotic, imbecile, mad, dazed; then with anything trifling, trivial, valued only by fools. From there, *fond* advanced to foolishly tender, doting; and finally to affectionate, with no reproach involved. To *fondle* is to caress; *fondlesome* describes a person given to fondling.

Fondant, as in confectionery, may be something you're fond of, but its origin is from French *fondre*, to melt, as in a cheese *fondue*.

fornicate

The Latin word *fornix* originally meant an arch or vault; and the word persists in scientific English today as a synonym for archlike. Anatomists use it to describe an arched formation of the brain; conchologists when talking of shell formations.

In ancient Rome, brothels were in a cave or under an arch, so the word *fornix* came to mean a brothel, and gave us the derivation of *fornicate*.

Technically there is a difference between *fornication* and *adultery*, *fornication* being defined as voluntary sexual intercourse between *unmarried* men and women; in *adultery*, at least one party is married. But I am reminded of the old story about the New England farmer who was asked about this distinction by his son. He answered: "Well, I've tried 'em both, and there ain't no difference." *Adultery* probably derives from the Latin *ad alter*, to another, and is not related to *adult* except by association in people's minds. *Adult* is from *adultus*, the past participle of *adolescere*, to grow up, as in our word *adolescent*.

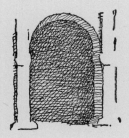

fraught

This verb is now generally a highfalutin, poetic term, used as in "fraught with care," but its real meaning is merely freight, from Middle Dutch *vracht*, freight, cargo, charge for same. It is identified with Old English *aéht*, acquisition, property, *aught*. The *London Gazette* of 1668, in its maritime notes, wrote: "The ships are said to be richly fraughted." *Freight* originally referred to cargo shipped by sea, not overland. In Scotland, *aucht*, meaning property, is a live word. *Aught*, in our sense of "anything whatever" is from Old English *àwiht*, creature, being, whit, thing.

Ought, the verb we use to express duty, in "you ought to do it," is from the same root, as are *owe* and *own*. *Ought* for cipher, zero, is a corruption of *nought*, nothing owned. The Class of Ought Nine in college should really be Nought Nine.

fruit

Whether you refer to fruits of the field or to the fruits of labor, they both come from Latin *frui*, to enjoy. *Fruition* is from the same root, and means enjoyment, pleasurable possession, and not, as it is frequently misused, ripening. The *fruition* of your work means your pleasure in it, not its maturing and bearing fruit, though that should be implicit.

The origins of some of our fruit names are interesting. *Grape*, for example, was the name of the instrument, a hook, used in grappling for the bunches—French *grape*, Teutonic *krappon*, Italian *grappo*, act of seizing, grabbing. *Peach* comes from Latin *Persicum pomum*, Persian apple. Since apples were the common denominator of fruit in all countries, all fruits at first were called apples of one sort or another. Consider the French potato—*pomme de terre*, earth apple; or love-apple, the earlier name for the tomato, held to be an aphrodisiac. The Anglo-Saxons called all fruit either apples or berries. *Pineapple* was so called because of its scaly resemblance to a pinecone. *Orange* is golden apple, from Sanskrit *naranga*.

Banana, a Spanish word, is probably from Arabic *banan*, a finger. *Cherry*, from French *cerise*, out of Greek, via Latin, *kerasion*, melon, from Cerasus in Pontus. The Greek *keras* means horn-bark, because a melon was as smooth as polished horn. Melon vines were brought from Armenia to Cantaloupo, the seat of the Pope near Rome— hence, *cantaloupe*. *Apricot* is probably from Latin *præco-*

quum, variant of *præcox*, early-ripe, ripe in summer, from the Latin prefix *præ*, before, and *coquere*, to cook. This delectable golden fruit, the apricot, is therefore related to *precocious*, flowering early, as does a prematurely developed child, a brat; and to *dementia præcox*, Latin *demens*, out of one's mind at an early age.

gadget

The origin of this handy word is obscure, but it is certainly not modern slang, as many people think, since it is said to have been current about 1870 among seafaring men. Some correspondents to the *Oxford Dictionary* say it was used in the fifties. One suggested etymology is French *gâchette*, a word applied to various pieces of mechanism; e.g., in a lock, in a gun. This is a diminutive of *gâche*, the staple of a lock, hook, etc. Or gadget may be connected with French *engager*, to engage one thing with another, interlocking. In French dialect *gagée* means tool or instrument. Robert Brown in *Spunyarn & Spindrift*, in 1886, wrote: "Then the names of all the other things on board a ship! I don't know half of them yet; even the sailors forget at times, and if the exact name of anything they want happens to slip from their memory, they call it a chicken-fixing, or a gadjet, or a gill-guy, or a timmey-noggy, or a wim-wam—just *pro tem.*, you know."

gag

This basic ration of stage and radio comedians is, as a word, an imitation of the sound made in choking or the sound of unmeaning chatter. In the 19th century, *gag-bills*, hand-bills, or throw-aways advertising the sensational episodes of a play were scattered around town in advance of the performance. Jerome K. Jerome, 1885, in *On the Stage*, wrote: "The old man has got the knack of making out good gag bills."

Later, *gags* came to mean expressions interpolated by the actor to funny up a slow situation. Perhaps this use developed from miners' slang, as this was the term for a bit of timber inserted temporarily in a mine-pit to keep two pieces of wood from settling.

A *gaggle* of geese, or of women, is an expression deriding the sound they make when all talk at once.

gas

This everyday word was coined by the Dutch chemist J. B. Van Helmont, who lived 1577–1644, and who may have modeled it on Dutch *geest*, spirit, since Van Helmont thought of *gas* as an occult principle contained in all bodies, an ultra-rarefied condition of water. He didn't know about cooking with *gas*, nor about *gas* in the slang sense of talking nonsense, "hot air," nor even about *gas* as short for gasoline.

ghetto

Having just finished John Hersey's great novel *The Wall*, I looked up *ghetto*. The *Oxford Dictionary* cautiously states that the word is Italian and that its etymology is guesswork, but that it is probably an abbreviation of *borghetto*, diminutive of *borgo*, borough, walled city. Old Teutonic *burg* meant shelter, fortress, castle, walled town, which we find in the suffixes of Edinburgh, Waterbury, Williamsburg. An author named Coryat wrote, in 1611, in *Crudities*: "The place where the whole fraternity of the Jews dwelleth together, which is called the Ghetto." A restricted area, originally found only in Italy, the *ghetto* soon spread to other lands. Figuratively the word means any segregated area, geographical or mental.

grocer

From Medieval Latin *grossarius*, from *grossus*, thick, big, gross. Originally a *grocer* was a wholesaler, one who bought and sold in the gross, the large. In London, the *Company of Grocers*, incorporated about 1344, were the lordly wholesale dealers in spice and foreign produce who set the ships a-sailing to import their wares from the East. *Gross* in its meaning of twelve dozen came into English via French.

grotesque

According to Florio, 1598, Italian *grottesca* was "a kinde of rugged unpolished painters worke, anticke worke," appropriate for decorating *grottos*, the popular name in Rome for vaulted chambers. These rooms, revealed by excavation in Pompeii, were sometimes taverns, sometimes brothels. (See *fornicate*.) This antique or anticke sense survives today in the murals of New York spaghetti joints. The sense of the meaning transferred itself from painting or sculpture of fantastic forms, foliage, and so forth, to anything ludricous because of incongruity, and finally to the fantastically absurd.

Grotto is from literary Latin *crypta*, from Greek *krypto*, to hide, a vault to hide in. From the same root we get *cryptic*, *cryptogram*, hidden writing or code, *crypto*, an unself-confessed Communist.

haberdasher

In my earlier book *In A Word*, I printed a charming derivation for this word which I have since learned is unauthenticated. I still admire it—the picture of a man going into a store and asking in German: *"Habt Ihr das?"*—"Do you have that?" The *Oxford Dictionary*, much less entertainingly, says that perhaps *haberdasher* is from Anglo-French *hapertas*, the name of a fabric—again, only perhaps. At any rate, *hapertas* occurs in an Anglo-French customs list of imported peltry, furs, and fabrics. The original prototype of President Harry S. Truman dealt in hats and caps.

ham

As applied to actors, this word has several folk-etymologies, none surely true. *Ham* is an old Teutonic word for crooked, the part of the leg that crooks, whether of a succulent porker or of a posturing actor. Another suggested etymology is that *ham* is a combination and abbreviation of two words—Cockney *h'amateur* plus *Hamlet*, the role all actors yearn to play. *Amateur* is French for one who does something for love, not pay, from Latin *amatorem*, lover. Still another suggested origin, given me by a theatrical friend, is that, before the days of cleansing cream in neat jars, when hamfat was used to remove make-up, an actor was called a *hamfatter* or *ham*. Cornelia Otis Skinner, in a *New Yorker* story of May 27, 1950, used the verb "hammed."

harum-scarum

A rhyming combination, apparently from hare, meaning to frighten, to harry, to hunt, a hare being notoriously timid; and scare. At first the expression was hare'em, scare'em. Similar formations are *hurry-scurry*, and *helter-skelter*, which vaguely imitates the hurried, heedless clatter of feet or hooves. Shakespeare in *Henry IV* said: "Helter-skelter have I rode to thee."

helicopter

This name for the most gentle and domesticated type of aircraft, the sort that flutters slowly to earth under its overhead propeller, was first used in 1872 in *Aeronaut*, to describe a model of a plane built by an airminded Frenchman, M. Pénaud. Jules Verne wrote in 1887, in *Clipper of the Clouds*: "We can look forward to such contrivances . . . which we can call streophores, helicopters, orthopters . . . by means of which man will become the master of space." Seen any streophores at LaGuardia Field lately? *Helicopter* is compounded of Greek *helix*, spiral, and *pteron*, wing.

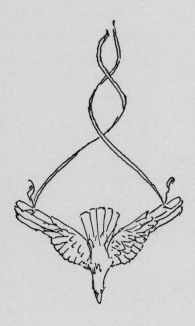

helium

This element of the catastrophic H-bomb is, in word-origin, purely benign, from the Greek *helios*, the sun. Some people, even today, believe it will bring us more blessing than destruction, since its energy is sunlike. *Helium* is one of the chemical elements, a transparent gas, first obtained in 1895 by Professor Ramsey. The *helium* bomb is also called the *hydrogen* bomb, *hydrogen* being one of the elements, coming from the Greek stems *hydro*, water, and *gen*, to be born, beget. It is a colorless, invisible, odorless gas, the lightest substance known, and it burns with a pale blue flame. It was formerly called "inflammable air." Water is the sole product of combustion of *hydrogen* in ordinary air, so perhaps the H-bomb will cure the New York water shortage—or drown us all.

Many other words are built on the combining form *heli-*, sun, among them the sunflower, *helianthus*, of which Jerusalem artichoke is also a species; *heliophobia* or dread of sunlight, disease of easy frecklers; *heliolatry*, sun worship—our summer sands are thick with heliolatrists. *Heliochrome* is a photograph in natural colors, forerunner of Glorious Technicolor. *Heliotrope* is a flower that turns to the sun.

hello

When an Old High German wanted to hail a ferryman, he yodeled *halâ* or *holâ*, which meant to fetch. The word in various times and places has been *hallo, halloa, hulla, hollo, hillo*. It has been a hunting-cry, and now is an almost global greeting or way to answer a telephone. The youngest generation has abridged it to "Hi!"

helot

When Byron wrote of "Slaves of the east, or helots of the West," he meant by *helots*, serfs or bondsmen; but the original *Helots* (with a capital) were the enslaved citizens of the town of Helos in Laconia. In order to teach the youth of Sparta that drunkenness is revolting, the Helots were used as graphic object lessons—they were forcibly fed more Spartan brew than they could well absorb, and then paraded in the public square to make an exhibition of themselves. Plutarch mentions a "drunken Helot," in his life of Lycurgus.

Hobson's choice

When you give a man Hobson's choice, you really give him no choice. It is a take-it-or-leave-it proposition. Who was Hobson and how did he make the dictionary? He was one Tobias H., a carrier and innkeeper of Cambridge, England, and *The Spectator*, No. 509, tells this story about him: "He kept a stable of forty good cattle, always ready and fit for travelling; but when a man came for a horse he was led into the stable, where there was great choice, but was obliged to take the horse which stood nearest to the stable-door; so that every customer was alike well served, according to his chance, and every horse ridden with the same justice."

hoosegow

This U.S. slang term for jail or lock-up is evolved from a perfectly dignified Mexican-Spanish word *juzgado*, past participle of *juzgar*, to judge. The criminal is judged, sentenced, jailed, all in one word. (The Spanish "j" is of course pronounced like "h.") Another slang name for jail, *jug*, is not an intimate way of saying *juzgado*, but is from *stone jug*, a deep smooth vessel from which you can't escape. The earliest known use in print is from *Niles' Weekly Register*, a U.S. publication, in 1815: "A full grown villain, who with an accomplice, were shortly after safely lodged in the jug"; though the term is defined earlier in a "vulgar" dictionary in England as "a nickname for Newgate Prison."

Clink, another name for a jail, comes out of London, too, and is not even termed slang by the *Oxford Dictionary*. Southwark, South of the Thames, across London Bridge of falling-down fame (though it never has, not even in the blitz), was in a district known as the *Liberty of the Clink*. There were four noted prisons there, of which one was called the *Clink*. It was not far from Shakespeare's Globe Theatre. An early guide-book of 1761, called *London & Environs*, says: "Clink prison in Clink Street, belongs to the liberty of the Bishop of Winchester, called the Clink liberty. . . . It is a very dismal hole where debtors are sometimes confined." The name may well have been, originally, descriptive, since one meaning of *clink* was to fasten securely, to *clinch*, to *clench*.

hormone

Hormones are as popular now in nonmedical speech as libido (q.v.) was a decade ago on the lips of the amateur psychiatrist. When your physician gives you a shot of hormones, he is, literally, stimulating your aging or sluggish faculties, since the word comes directly from Greek *hormon*, present participle of *horman*, to urge on, to impel, to set in motion. First written use of the term, according to the *Oxford Dictionary* was in 1905 in *Lancet*, where E. H. Starling wrote: "These chemical messengers, however, or 'hormones' . . . as we might call them." They are messengers in the sense that a substance formed in one endocrine organ is carried by the blood stream to another, which it stimulates.

impeccable

From Latin *impeccare*, not to sin. An *impeccable* character is one incapable of sinning, faultless, unerring; and a
man or woman who is *impeccably* dressed is style-perfect—
not a button loose, nor a tie unmatched. *Peccable* means
capable of sinning; as who isn't? No one ever seems to use
this positive word. A *peccadillo* is a tiny, diminutive sin
or fault.

Peculation is sinning on a grander scale—embezzlement,
no less—but the root of the word is not the same. *Peculate*
is from Latin *peculium*, private property, from *pecu*, cattle,
since your wealth was once gauged by the number of
head of cattle you owned. *Impecunious* is to own no sheep
or cows. *Fee*, what a lawyer charges you, came by its meaning similarly but from Anglo-Saxon *feoh*, the word for
cattle. I have always been rather regretful that my husband, who is a lawyer, isn't paid in Jerseys, so many head
for a divorce, so many for a censorship case, maybe a
heifer or two for a tax return. (Irrelevant intelligence: the
cows on the Isle of Jersey are all buttoned into topcoats in
December.)

implicit

From Latin *implicatus, implicate,* entangle, involve, from the earlier Latin *implicare,* to fold or twist in. Milton, in *Paradise Lost,* uses *implicit* in this early literal sense of entangled when he writes: "The humble Shrub, And bush with frizl'd hair implicit." He didn't mean that the bush was unquestioning, but that its twigs were all entangled in each other.

Implicit faith was a term from ecclesiastical Latin meaning faith in spiritual matters, not independently arrived at by the individual, but involved in the general belief of the Church. Hence, our use of *implicit* as synonym for unquestioning, absolute, as in the expressions *implicit* confidence, *implicit* belief, *implicit* obedience.

To *imply* is to fold in a meaning, an etymology that ought to clarify affairs for those who confuse *imply* and *infer,* which means to carry in. *Explicit* is open out, unfolded, therefore clear and definite. *Duplicity* means twice folded, double-dealing, and a *duplicate* is something folded twice, or twofold. A *duplex* is a double-storied apartment.

inchoate

Through some sound-connection with *chaos* and *chaotic*, people use this word as if it meant utter confusion and disorder. It doesn't, except that things just begun, incipient, may be incidentally upset. *Inchoate* is from Latin *incohare*, to begin. An *inchoate* plan is not necessarily a confused one; it is merely elementary, undeveloped, therefore imperfect. *Chaos* is from the Greek word meaning a gaping void, a yawning gulf, chasm, or the nether abyss, the first state of the universe. It is a rather awesome picture in the Velikovsky *Worlds in Collision* style, and seems too large a word to apply to a topsy-turvy bureau drawer or a desk. *Chasm* is from the same stem, meaning yawning, hollow.

indomitable

An *indomitable* spirit is like a determinedly wild beast—
it cannot be tamed. This word comes from Latin *indo-
mitare,* not tamed. We might call a dog or a horse a *dom-
itable* animal. Perhaps there is a relationship with *domi-
nate,* Latin *dominari,* to govern, lord it, rule, and the
other words from this root—*dominus,* lord or master;
anno Domini, year of the Lord; *dominatrix,* mistress;
domineer, lord it over, bully; *dominion,* lands ruled by a
master; and *dominie,* a schoolmaster in J. M. Barrie's
stories or in Scotland generally.

inept

From Latin *inaptus*, not apt, unfitted, unsuited, inappropriate, past participle of *apere*, to fasten, or attach. The *inept* person is thus one who is unfastened, unattached, and therefore not quick to learn. The *ept* person—except that we say *apt*—is quick-witted and ready to learn. *Apt* has come to mean customarily disposed to do something. We say: "It's apt to rain in April." Pope, in *The Iliad*, wrote: "For apt is youth to err." An *aptitude* test indicates at what trade or profession a student will be *apt*. *Adapt* means to fit or make suitable.

inert

Like inept, this is another word we use only in the negative, though once *ert* was used as a synonym for to be eager, to hurry, to incite, to urge on, encourage, or irritate and provoke. A useful word, and I regret its obsolescence. You could *ert* on a lazy horse, or say to an impatient husband: "Don't ert me, I have to put on my lipstick." As late as 1789 D. Davidson, in *Seasons*, wrote: "The herd . . . now and then Erts on the tir'd tike with 'Sheep awa, a, a!'" The origin of *ert* is probably Old Norse *erta*, to taunt, tease.

inkling

From Middle English *nyngkiling,* recorded once only, to
whisper. In my previous book, *In A Word,* I said that
inkling is now used only in the negative in phrases such
as: "I haven't an inkling," meaning: "I haven't even a
hint as to the idea." And I complained because the use of
inkle as a verb has become obsolete. Four readers wrote
in to correct me, and to state that *inkle* is a term used in
bridge, a game about which I obviously know nothing.
For example, a declarer "inkles a spade," which is a warn-
ing to his partner that he can't count on much. He has
just a hint of spades.

isotope

I thought this a brand-new word that accompanied atomic science, but it seems to have been coined in 1913 by Professor Frederick Soddy from Greek *isos*, equal, and *topos*, place. A better word would have been *homotope*, same place, since *isotopes* represent elements or atoms occupying the same position in the periodic table.

jackanapes

The precise origin of this contemptuous term is uncertain, but it was first used as a nickname—uncomplimentary—for William de la Pole, Duke of Suffolk, murdered in 1450, whose badge was a clog and a chain such as were attached to a tame ape. In a poem of the time, Suffolk was styled "the Ape-clogge," and was later referred to as an ape called *Jack Napes*. Perhaps Napes is from Naples, since monkeys were often exhibited by Italian showmen, just as they are now.

jeep

When the United States Army in World War II ordered the automotive engineers to build for them a General Purpose car, it was designated by the initials G.P., which in short order became "jeep." Just so the Vice President, Alben Barkley, has become affectionately known as the Veep. Both words have a tender, diminutive connotation to our ears, perhaps from association with the peep of baby birds or the cheep of infant chicks.

Here are the name-origins of some other vehicles: car, via the Latin *carrus*, from Old Celtic *karros*, a two-wheeled wagon or *chariot*; *char-a-banc*, in French, a car with a bench, in modern days a busful of jolly British trippers. *Bus* is short for *omnibus*, Latin dative plural of *omnia*, all, meaning literally "for all." *Cab* is an abbreviation of *cabriolet*, so called because it bounds about like a goat. *Capro* is Italian for goat, whence *Capri*, goat-island, and *capricious*. *Coupé* is just French for cut off, a shortened car. *Phaeton*, once an open carriage, later an open touring-car, was named for the unlucky son of Apollo, the Sun-God, who drove his father's chariot across the sky to his death. A few quaint and delightful *Hansom cabs* are still for hire at the south side of Central Park in New York. These duplex vehicles were patented in 1834 by an architect named Hansom. Disraeli called them the gondolas of London.

jeopardy

Middle English *iuparti*, Old French *ieu* (*jeu*) *parti*, literally, divided play or game, whence comes our meaning of uncertain chance, uncertainty, risk. At first, the term was used in chess or similar games, but by Chaucer's day it had come to mean, in a general sense, risk, peril of harm or death. *Double jeopardy*—to try a man twice for the same offense, once he has been acquitted—is illegal in the United States.

jeroboam

In I Kings xi, 28, *Jeroboam* was "a mighty man of valour," who, three verses later, "made Israel to sin." Since an over-sized bottle of wine, or a very large goblet, can cause sin, too, it is called a *jeroboam*. Sir Walter Scott used the word in *The Black Dwarf*: "Or make a brandy jeroboam in a frosty morning."

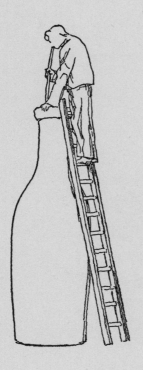

jeunesse dorée

Now generally a somewhat literary term for highly privileged young people of wealth and fashion, this expression was originally applied in France to a group of elegant counter-revolutionaries who banded together after the fall of Robespierre. It is a French phrase meaning gilded youth. Carlyle, in *The French Revolution*, writes: "Fréron, in his fondness, names them Jeunesse Dorée, Golden, or Gilt Youth."

jinx

Jinx is not a modern slang word for dogging ill-luck, but a very ancient one. This was the Greek name for a bird, known to us as the wryneck, made use of in witchcraft to cast a charm or spell on the selected victim. The wryneck has a harsh cry—as who wouldn't with a twisted neck?—which sounds like a triple "Jinx." The Greeks spelled it with a "y."

jitney

Some twenty-five years ago, when taxi licensing was less strict than it is today, all over the United States fleets of rattletrap cheap taxicabs were in operation. In many small towns, they would deliver a passenger, more or less intact, for a nickel. They were called *jitneys*. The *Oxford Dictionary* says the origin of the word is uncertain; but the *Nation*, New York, of February 4, 1915, has this to offer: "The word jitney . . . is the Jewish slang term for a nickel." The discussion went on in the March 18 issue, with this addition: "A *jitney* bus derives its name from *jitney*, meaning the smallest coin in circulation in Russia."

Kilkenny cats

There is a fable in Kilkenny, in Leinster, Eire, about two embattled cats who fought each other so bitterly that, at the end, only the tails remained. We use the expression to describe combatants who fight until they annihilate each other.

kith and kin

Kith is from Old Teutonic *kunþ*, known; Old English cuð, couth, and originally meant knowledge, acquaintance with someone or something, information. The word went through many meanings. At one time it meant rules of etiquette, how to behave, a sort of Emily Post book of the Middle Ages. Next, it denoted a country or place that is known, familiar; one's native land. Still later, it came to mean known or familiar persons, collectively—friends, neighbors, fellow countrymen; and it was at this stage in its life history that *kith* became utterly tangled with *kin*, so that nowadays they are used as synonyms. "Kith and kin" originally meant "country and kinsfolk." A *kithless* man was one without friends, poor wight.

Kin came to us via Old Teutonic, from the Aryan stem *gen-*, to produce, beget, as in Latin *genus*, race or stock, kind, gender, sex, and so means family or blood-relatives. *Kindred* is from the same root, as is *kind*, used as a noun. The adjective *kind* once meant natural, native, of good birth. Those of good birth were supposed to be generous and gentle, or *kind*, a sort of "noblesse oblige" idea.

knickerbocker

This word, now a synonym for New York City or a name for blousy knee-pants little boys wore before the day of shorts and jeans, comes from a Dutch word *knikker*, a marble used in schoolboy play, and *bocker*, baker of the clay marble. In Dutch, *knicken* means to crack or snap, onomatopœic for the sound of marbles clicking together. As late as 1860, to play "knickers" in New York was to shoot marbles.

Washington Irving called his pretended author of his *History of New York* Diedrich Knickerbocker, and so popularized the name. Cruikshank illustrated the first edition with Dutchmen in loose-fitting, blousy knee-breeches, which quickly came to be known as *knickerbockers* or *knickers*. I believe English girls wear a combination undergarment advertised as "camiknickers."

To go back to marbles for a moment, the origin of *taw*, that "aggie" prize of your shooter's collection, with which he makes his shot, is unknown, but Steele in *The Tatler*, in 1709, mentions it: "He is hiding or hoarding his Taws and Marbles." *Marble* itself is from Latin *marmor*, cognate with a Greek word meaning shining or sparkling stone. *Taw* also means the line from which the player shoots, and has been confused with "toe the line."

labor

Latin *laborem* meant toil, distress, trouble, and not *labor* in our sense of exertion of body or mind, often painful or compulsory. Adam Smith in *The Wealth of Nations* (1776) first used the word in the modern sense of physical exertion directed to the supply of the material wants of the community.

Laboratory, a place to work, and *elaborate,* an example of art or craftsmanship much worked over, come from the same root. In the expression "in labor"—childbirth pains —we go back to the Latin origin.

Travail, also meaning toil, long painful effort, is from the French word for work. *Travel* comes from the same root, since before the days of cars and trains and planes, *traveling* was a painful and long-drawn-out suffering; and *travel* was a synonym for hard labor, as Hakluyt uses it in his *Voyages:* "Some cut hoops, others laboured upon the sails and ship, every man travelling for his life."

A *travail,* according to an early dictionary, was "the frame whereinto Farriers put unrulie horses, when they shooe or dresse them." Perhaps the root is Latin *trabs,* beam, or perhaps *trepalium,* a three-staked instrument of torture. If the latter is true, the sense development passed from to torture; to afflict, harass, weary; to toil, labor; and finally, to travel.

ledger

A *ledger*, forbiddingly arithmetical tome familiar to every office, should be by the very nature of its origin a cumbersome volume. The word is probably formed on Old English *leggen*, dialect form of lie or lay, and originally meant "a book that lies permanently in some place," too heavy to move around or hold.

The *Wriothesley Chronicle*, 1538, says: "The curates should provide a booke of the bible in Englishe, of the largest volume, to be a lidger in the same church for the parishioners to read on." There are two other specialized meanings of *ledger*: a horizontal timber in scaffolding; and a resident ambassador. The base word *lie* is from Latin *lectus*, bed.

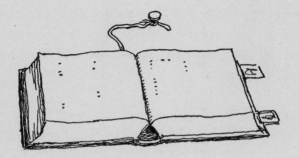

let

One of those anomalous words in English where we find a single root growing into two homonyms of directly opposite meaning. We have *let* meaning to allow, to permit, and *let* meaning to hinder, to prevent. They are both from Teutonic *laet*, related to *late*, whence Latin *lassus*, weary, as in *lassitude*. The primary sense of the verb seems to be "to let go through weariness, to neglect," as when you give in to some demand because you are too bored to say "no" again. Marriages are occasionally the result of this state of mind.

Let is used in the opposite sense, that of to prevent, in the phrase "without let or hindrance." In tennis, a "let ball" must be served again.

libido

This psychoanalytic term, now glibly on the lips of the layman, was first used by Jung in 1913, in his book *Psychoanalysis*. In 1922, Freud, in *Group Psychology*, defined it thus: "Libido is an expression taken from the theory of the emotions. We call by that name the energy . . . of those instincts which have to do with all that may be comprised under the word *love*." The origin is Latin *libido*, meaning desire, lust, the sense retained in *libidinous*.

The word *love*, while Teutonic, has an older Aryan root represented in Latin *lubet* (*libet*), it is pleasing. *Lubh* was Sanskrit for "to desire."

lido

This is the Italian word for a shore or beach. The most famous and fashionable in Italy, near Venice, became known as *"The" Lido*—a fine wide stretch of dirty-looking lava dust—and *Lido* has now become the term for every Long Island overcrowded beach, swimming-pool, and other place of only remotely aquatic entertainment.

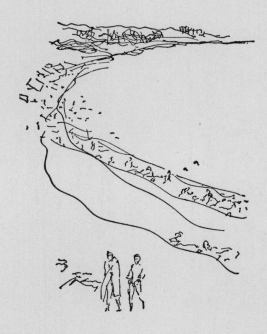

lieutenant

From two French words, *lieu*, place, and *tenant*, holding, an officer of lower grade who takes the place of a captain. The British *subaltern* is Latin *subalter*, under another. The English pronunciation of *lieutenant* (looey in our army) as "leftenant" is due to an early printing confusion of "u" with "v" or "f." Another term for a deputy or substitute, frequently used for a minister or doctor temporarily filling a pulpit or an office, is *locum tenens*, Latin for "one who holds the place."

maladroit

A *maladroit* man is one wanting in adroitness, awkward, bungling, clumsy, the one who always knocks over the highball glass or cuts himself while shaving. *Maladroit* is from two French words, *mal*, ill and *à droit*, rightly; in other words, wrong. *Droit*, in turn, is from Latin *dirigere*, to straighten, set straight, direct.

There is a parallel between *direct* and *address*. *Dress* is from the same root, and when you put your clothes on, you make yourself right or ready. When a military order is given to "dress ranks," the officer expects every foot, eye, and weapon to be in order. When a father administers a "dressing down" to his son, he is setting him to rights—at least in Pop's opinion. A hairdresser puts your locks in order. Shakespeare first used dress as a noun synonym for costume. And food was originally dressed or made ready on a sideboard called a *dresser*.

manger

A cafeteria for cattle, this word is directly from the French *manger* to eat. Interestingly enough, the proverbial *dog in the manger*, who doesn't want to eat hay or oats but prevents others from doing so, is in the parallel French proverb *Le chien du jardinier*, the gardener's dog, who wouldn't dream of eating cabbages but keeps any one else away from them. Speaking of dogs, the skin-disease *mange* is from the same root, through French, from Latin *mandere*, to chew, itch.

marmalade

When we have toast and *marmalade* for breakfast, we generally eat *orange marmalade*, although the Portuguese word *marmelo* means quince, and came from the Greek *melimelon*, honey-apple, a kind of apple and quince graft. Henry VIII in his *Letters* mentions "one box of marmalade . . . presented by Hull of Exeter." I assume he meant preserves, though maybe not, considering Hal's reputation—in Henry's day a "marmalade-madam" was another word for a strumpet. *Marmalade cats* are of course yellow and white. "Orlando" is a charming *marmalade* feline in English children's fiction.

Allied words in the confection field are: *jelly*, which is from Latin *gelata*, frozen, *congealed*, and *gelatin*. In Italy, the equivalent of Good Humor men call out: *"Gelata!"* to advertise their ice-cream sticks. *Jam* is onomatopœic, akin to *champ*, the sound of crushing or squeezing the fruit to a pulp.

meat

From an Old Teutonic word *matiz*, "meat" originally meant any solid food. *Green meat* was vegetables. An interesting chapter of English history is wrapped up in our dual terms for certain meats, dating from the Norman Conquest. After the defeat of Harold at Hastings, Britain was an occupied area, and the Saxons, deprived of land and wealth, no longer able to afford much meat for their trenchers, became the husbandmen of livestock to supply the joints for the Conqueror's table. Thus we retained the Old English word for an animal on the hoof, and acquired the Norman French name for it as it appeared, steaming, at the table. These bilingual pairs are: *cow* as opposed to *beef*; *sheep* and *lamb*, as contrasted with French *mutton*; *calf* and *veal*; *pig* and *ham*; *deer* and *venison*.

Modern French has borrowed back *beef*, which appears on French menus as *biftek* and *rosbif*, instead of the French *bœuf*.

At official ceremonies or parades in London you will see the *Beefeaters* in their 15th century scarlet uniforms. These are the King's Yeomen of the Guard, an organization instituted at the accession of Henry VII in 1485. The term "beef-eaters" was, at first, contemptuously used for a well-fed menial.

For a splendidly written and moving story of the Norman Conquest, read Hope Muntz's *The Golden Warrior*. *Venison*, incidentally, came into English via Norman

French from the Latin *venari*, to hunt, and originally embraced the flesh of any animal, used as food, killed in the chase—not only deer, but wild boar, hare, rabbit, and bear.

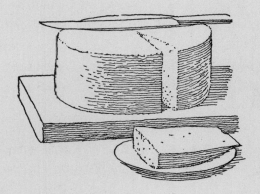

Mercury

The trim little gilt-bronze god with the winged heels and the G.I. helmet who presides over traffic on New York's Fifth Avenue was, originally, only the Roman god of commerce, and derived his name, probably, from Latin *merx*, merchandise. It was later in Roman literature that he became identified with the Greek messenger of the gods, Hermes, a young fellow with innumerable jobs—he was the god of eloquence and feats of skill; protector of traders and thieves; road supervisor; conductor of departed souls to the lower world. The liquid metal *quicksilver* is called *mercury* because it flies about so incredibly fast. Ever try to recapture the *mercury* from a broken thermometer? From the same root we get *mercurial*, a fast-rising or -falling temperament, *merchant*, *merchandise*, *commerce*, trading together, and *mercer*, a dealer in textiles.

minuet

This slow and stately measure, danced with short small steps, is in French *menuet*, diminutive of *menu*, small, which is in turn derived from Latin *minutus*, past participle of *minuere*, to make small, diminish. A *menu* or list of dishes to be served is so called because of the sense of small detail in such a list. In 17th-century France, a common expression was "menu peuple," the little people, Henry Wallace's patronizing "common man," often abbreviated to "the Menu."

We have many other words from the same origin: *minor*, to make less, the lesser; *minorite*, a Friar Minor, a Franciscan monk; *miniscule*, a small letter; *diminish*; and *minus*. *Minus* as we use it in mathematics did not occur in Latin at any period, and the terms *plus* and *minus*, with the symbols $+$, $-$, were first used by merchants in Germany, about the 15th century, to mark excess or deficiency in weights and measures. In a 1489 book on commercial arithmetic the symbols occur for the first time in print, in this sense.

Minute is cognate with *minor*, and indicates a tiny part of a unit—a sixtieth part of an hour, or one degree of a circle. The *minutemen* of the American Revolution were militia ready for instant service. *Minutes* of a meeting originally referred to a rough copy in *small* writing as distinguished from the *engrossed* document.

The small size characteristic of paintings in *miniature* has led to a pseudo-etymological association with the

Latin root *min-*, expressing smallness. The real meaning
of *miniature* has nothing to do with size, since it comes
from Latin *miniare*, to illuminate a manuscript, to ru-
bricate or paint with vermilion. Strictly speaking, a *miniature poodle* is not a tiny dog but a brightly colored pup.
However, confusion in usage has now established the
word *miniature* as a synonym for very small.

miscreant

A creature of opprobrium frequently met with in romances of the Middle Ages, a *miscreant* is heretical, infidel, depraved, villainous—simply because he does not believe in your doxy (the ortho one), your religion, or your standards of conduct. The word means, literally, to misbelieve, from the Latin *miscredere*, not to believe. *Creant*, most contrarily, does not mean believing, but in the phrase "to cry creant" is an admission that one gives up, is vanquished. Perhaps related to *craven*.

moot

A question that can be argued, which is debatable and doubtful, is a "moot question." The origin lies in Old English *mot*, meaning encounter, meeting, assembly—in fact, *meet* is a derivative. The national council or parliament of Anglo-Saxon England was called the Assembly of Old Wise Men—the *Witenagemot*—and various courts of justice were called Gemot, Burgh-Mote, Folk-Mote, Hall-Mote, Hundred-Mote, and so on.

Another obsolete use of *moot* was as a synonym for "dig up by the roots," or "unearth an otter."

Today, law schools hold *moot court*, a court at which, for practice, the students argue imaginary cases, often hypothetical doubtful cases used for discussion.

mugwump

This is a U.S. term for one who stands aloof from politics, the man who can't make up his mind whether he's a Democrat or a Republican; a fence-sitter. In popular definition, a guy who has his *mug* on one side of the fence and his *"wump"* on the other. The word was originally *mugquomp* in American Indian, Algonkian, and meant "great chief." It is used in Eliot's Massachusetts Bible, published in 1663, to translate the English title "duke," and was used to give the Indians a conception of such chiefs as Joshua, or Gideon, or Joab. (Fiske: *Beginnings of New England.*)

Specifically, in American politics, a *mugwump* was an adherent of the Republican Party who, in the Presidential election of 1884, in the avowed interest of civil-service reform, declined to support the nominee of his party, James G. Blaine, and either voted the Democratic or Prohibition ticket, or refrained from voting at all.

names

Most parents choose names for their babies because they like the sound of a special aggregation of letters, or because they want to give brief immortality to a grandparent or a friend, with no consideration—and indeed no knowledge—of the name's meaning. Yet every name has a derivation. In the ancient days, the Hebrews, the Greeks, the Romans, the Celts, the Anglo-Saxons, called a child by the noun or adjective that described him or was a hope for the qualities he might possess on growing up. Now that we have lost this art of appropriate nomenclature, how often do our first names fit us?

Let's take the names of the President and his Cabinet (as of May, 1950): *Harry*, Teutonic, home lord. (Very apt.) *Alben*, Latin, fair. *Dean*, Latin, deacon. *Charles* (two of them), Teutonic, strong. *Louis*, Teutonic, famed fighter—good name for the Secretary of Defense. *Oscar*, Celtic, leaping warrior. *John*, Hebrew, the Lord is gracious, or gift of God. *Howard*, Teutonic, castle guard. *Jesse*, Hebrew, wealthy. *Maurice*, Latin, dark, Moorish.*

Here are more names for Baby: *Abner*, Hebrew, my father is a lamp. *Adolph*, Teutonic, noble wolf. *Adrian*, Latin, black earth. *Ahern*, Celtic, lord of horses. *Ada*, Hebrew, ornament. *Agnes*, Greek, lamb. *Alden*, Teutonic, old town. *Alfred*, Teutonic, elf counsel. *Algernon*, Celtic, bearded. *Arabella*, Latin, fair refuge. *Cecil*, Latin, blind. *Claude*, Latin, lame. *Cyrus*, Persian, sun. *Cordelia*, Celtic,

* In September: for *Louis*, substitute *George*, Greek, farmer.

jewel of the sea. *Cornelia*, Latin, crowned. *Dwight*, Teutonic, wise fellow. *Geraldine*, Teutonic, little one with the bold spear. *Graham*, Celtic, stern-faced. *Hilary*, Latin, merry, hilarious. *Hiram*, Hebrew, lofty. *Horace*, Latin, keen-eyed. *Hulda*, Hebrew, weasel. *Jennifer*, Celtic, white wave. *Julius*, Latin, blond-bearded. *Keith*, Celtic, windy. *Leah*, Hebrew, languid. *Lucretia*, Latin, lucky. *Meredith*, Celtic, sea-guardian. *Napoleon*, Greek, lion of the new city. *Neil*, Celtic, champion. *Otis*, Greek, keen of ear. *Philip*, Greek, lover of horses. *Priscilla*, Latin, old-fashioned. *Quentin*, Latin, fifth son. *Ross*, Teutonic, steed. *Russell*, Teutonic, red-haired. *Sophie*, Greek, wisdom *Ursula*, Latin, little bear. *Zoë*, Greek, life.

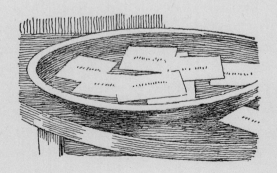

nonchalant

The nonchalant person is cool and indifferent, unenthusiastic, a literal etymology, since the word is from French *nonchaloir*, not heated, derived from Latin *noncalere*, not to be hot. *Calor* is Latin for heat, from which we get *calorie*, the amount of food needed to heat you or energize you.

nonplus

A Latin phrase meaning "not more," "no further." When you are *nonplussed*, you are in a state of perplexity or puzzlement, in which no more can be said or done. You don't know how to proceed or what to say. The original Latin phrase was *"non plus ultra"* or *"ne plus ultra,"* "(let there) not (be) more (sailing) beyond," alleged to have been inscribed on the Pillars of Hercules, beyond which no ship could safely sail. The Pillars of Hercules are an ancient tower at Corunna in Spain, supposed to have been a Roman Pharos or lighthouse, and the furthermost limit of safe pre-Columbus navigation.

nympholepsy

Nympha is Greek for nymph or bride, and *nympholepsy* is a state of rapture supposed to be inspired in men by nymphs; hence, an ecstasy or frenzy of emotion, especially if inspired by something unattainable. The most striking modern example is Harpo Marx when he tries to climb up every tall, unattainable blonde he sees in every Marx Brothers' movie. A *nympholept* is a man caught by nymphs, and filled by violent enthusiasm for them. Two pleasant words for a young or little nymph are *nymphet* and *nymphlin*.

Nymphomania, nymph madness, is a feminine disease of disturbed eroticism, morbid and uncontrollable sexual desire for any and every man.

odd

An odd little round word, originally *The Third Man* (but
without zither music), it comes from Old Norse *odda-
maðr*, odd man, third man, who gives the deciding vote.
Oddi meant point, angle, or triangle, whence third or *odd*
number. The root is also that of point, a certain spot. The
sense extended from the third or unpaired member of a
group of three to any single or unpaired member of a
group, as in "three's a crowd." An umpire, in Scottish,
used to be an *oddsman*, and his female counterpart an
oddwoman.

omelet

The puffy eiderdown-quilt *omelet* served by Madame Poularde of Mont St. Michel belies the origin of the word. *Omelet* is from Old French *lamelle* and Latin *lamella*, diminutive of *lamina*, thin plate, blade of a sword or knife, descriptive of the thin, flat type of *omelet*, practically a pancake.

From the same root, we get the science term *lamina*, a thin plate, scale, or layer; and *laminated*, built up layer upon layer like a fine cake or veneer. Mrs. S. Harrison, the Rombauer or Fannie Farmer of 1748, wrote in her *House-keeper's Pocket-Book* of "Eggs dress'd, in several sorts of Amlets." The proverb, "Omelets cannot be made without breaking eggs," is of French origin.

orchid

This exotic dream flower gets its name, according to Pliny, from *orchis*, Greek word for testicle, because of the resemblance of tubers to the male organ. Indeed, *orchotomy* is the medical term for castration. This entire line of etymology would be a distinct surprise to the girls who wear the flowers; or at any rate to some of them. The *orchis* is first mentioned in an English herbal of 1562, by Turner, who says: "There are diuers kindes of orchis . . . yᵉ other kindes ar in other countrees called fox stones or hear stones, and they may after yᵉ Greke be called dogstones." Tennyson, in *In Memoriam*, says: "Bring orchis, bring the foxglove spire, The little speedwell's darling blue." Some of the common names of *orchids* describe the animal or thing the flower is supposed to resemble: Bee, Bird's-nest, Butterfly, Cuckoo, Finger, Fly, Frog, Greenman, Lizard, Medusa's-head, Monkey, Spider.

ostracize

From the Greek *ostrakon,* shell, later an earthen vessel, tile, or potsherd, because of the ancient Greek punishment of banishing a man by writing his name on a shell or a bit of earthen tile. *Ostracism* was temporary banishment from Athens. A citizen whose power was considered dangerous to the state was sent into exile for ten years, his judges writing their votes on shells or potsherds and dropping them into a Keatsian urn. *Oyster,* with his hard shell, is from the same Greek root.

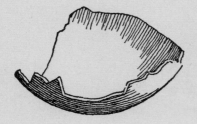

overwhelm

Why are we never whelmed by waves or events or emotions, but always *over*whelmed? *Whelm* is from Old Norse *hvalf*, a vault or concavity, and is related to the Greek word for bosom, the radical notion being of something rounded or arched. Old Norse *hvalfa* meant to capsize, to turn a vessel upside down so that its rounded bottom was uppermost. There is a Scottish dialect word, *whemmel*, which means an upset, an upheaval.

pall

Figuratively, we speak of a *pall* falling over a room, a crowd, a scene, as though a cloud or smoke shut out the brightness. A *pall* is something that covers or conceals, producing an effect of gloom. Literally, the word means a costly cloak or robe, often purple, and is from Old English *pæl*, an adaption of Latin *pallium*, coverlet, curtain, cloak; a Greek mantle, the philosopher's cloak.

In early Britain, *pall* was fine or rich material, as used for robes of rank, or in ecclesiastical use, for an altar-cloth or a purple cover for a coffin. Hence, *pallbearers* at a funeral.

It is difficult to trace the relationship, which does exist, with the verb *to pall*, meaning to become tasteless, insipid, to appetite or interest, through over-use. The verb is derived from Old French *appall*, to wax pale with fright, pallor as seen through a cloud, to be in consternation.

Pall Mall

London's fine, broad street, center of fashionable club
life, gets its name from an Italian game, *palla-maglio*, literally ball-mallet. The game was widely popular in the
16th century in Italy, France, and Scotland, and in England in the 17th. A boxwood ball was driven through an
iron ring suspended at some height above ground in a long
grassy alley, which became known as *The Mall*, because
there the gallants swung their *mallets*. Pepys, in his *Diary*
for April 2, 1661, writes: "To St. James's Park, where I
saw the Duke of York playing at Pelemele, the first time
that ever I saw the sport."

pantry

Not a room for pans and pots, but originally a storeroom for bread. It is derived from Latin *panetus*, a little loaf of bread. Nor is the *buttery* a place for butter. It was a storeroom for casks or *butts* of wine; from Latin *botaria*, a wine-vessel, Late Latin *butta*, a wine-skin. A *butt* holds anywhere from 108 to 140 gallons, though the earlier size must have been much smaller, as there is a note in Roger's *Agriculture and Prices*, 1443, that a "Rhenish 1 butt = 36 gals." Shakespeare is always talking about a "butt of malmsey."

Bottle has the same root, and so does *butler*, the servant who has charge of the wine cellar and who dispenses the liquor. Authority does not know, nor venture to guess, why a *hogshead* became a measure for liquid entertainment. How much would a hog's head hold, anyway?

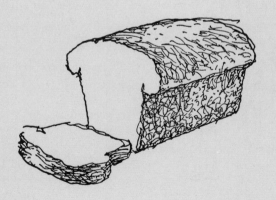

paradise

This heavenly word is from Old Persian *pairidaeza*, an enclosure or park. In Late Hebrew it was *pardēs*, used to designate the royal forest of King Artaxerxes, to whom Nehemiah went for timber "to make beams for the gates of the palace." The Hebrew word for *paradise* in Ecclesiastes is thus translated in detail by King James's Bible-writers: "I made me gardens and orchards, and I planted trees in them of all kind of fruits: I made me pools of water . . . I got me servants and maids . . . I got me men singers and women singers, and the delights of the sons of men." Truly, *paradise!*

In modern Persian and Arabic the word has become *firdaus*, a garden. Xenophon first used the word in Greek in describing a Persian enclosed park or pleasure ground. *Paradise* did not attain its present meaning as the abode of the blessed until the New Testament Christian writers so construed it. The Garden of Eden was the earthly *Paradise*, as distinguished from the celestial.

Chaucer said: "Wedlok is so esy and so clene that in this world it is a Paradys." That state of illusory happiness known as a *fool's paradise* was so called in English letters as early as the 15th century. *Fool*, incidentally, comes from Latin *follis*, bellows, windbag.

paramount

A matter of *paramount* importance is of supreme or superior importance; a *paramount* chief is one at the top in the scale of rank or authority. This word had no such meaning in its origin, but was a simple indication of something *above* another in physical position. For example, a writer might refer to a *paramount* sentence on a page, meaning merely a sentence higher up. The word came into English via Old French *par á mont*, upward, which in turn was derived from Latin *ad montem*, to the mount or hill.

pavilion

In Old French of the 12th century, *paveillun* was a tent, a canopy, gaily set up in all its rich blaze of color to shelter knights and ladies at the jousting. These *pavilions* were as gauzy and as brilliant as butterfly wings, which is precisely the derivation of the word—Latin *papilonum*, butterfly. Later, a *pavilion* was any light ornamental building or pleasure-house set up in parks or public gardens.

How the word came to mean anything so dour and unpleasurable as the wing of a hospital is difficult to trace, but the meaning was already established by 1859 when Florence Nightingale, in her *Notes on Hospitals*, remarked that the hospitals in France and Belgium were "divided into separate pavilions."

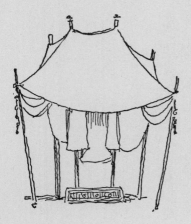

pedagogue

No teacher likes to be called a *pedagogue* (and I was one long enough to know), with its more or less contemptuous modern implication of pedantry and severe stuffiness. The word in its derivative sense did not even mean a teacher, but described the servant who led the well-to-do Greek boy to school. Its roots are the Greek *pai(d-)s*, child, and *agō*, to lead.

Pediatrics is derived from the Greek word for child and *iaomai*, to heal. Two other words built on the *agō* root, to lead, are *synagogue*, meaning to lead together, a meeting or assembly place; and *demagogue*, now used in a derogatory sense as a leader of the mob, a political agitator, a rabble-rouser, though in ancient Athens a *demagogue* was a fine, upstanding leader of the people, a popular leader or orator championing the common citizenry.

pedigree

From French *pié* (*pied*) *de grue*, a crane's foot. So called from a three-line mark ⅄ used in denoting succession in *pedigrees*, whether of men, champion dogs, or Derby winners. This conventional mark used in genealogical tables resembles the claws of a bird, more particularly the long, bony foot of a crane as he stands in his marsh meditating on frogs and fish.

The family tree of the root *pes, pedem,* Latin for foot, is wide-branching. A few of the descendants are: *pedal,* a lever worked by foot; *pedestal,* the foot or base of something; *pedestrian,* on foot or one who walks; *pedicle,* a botanical small foot or stalk; *pedicular,* pertaining to the many-footed louse; *pedicure,* care of feet; *pediform,* foot-shaped; *pediluvium,* a foot-bath; *pedissequent,* one who follows on foot; *peddler* or *pedlar,* a word of obscure origin—it may have meant a man who trudged the roads selling his wares, or it may have come from the pack he carried, since a *ped,* in the Eastern Counties in England, is a wicker pannier. A *pedometer* measures the steps you take on a hike; and a *centipede* has—more or less—a hundred feet. For more relatives, see *expedite.*

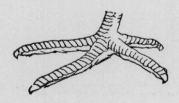

penicillin

One of our newer miracles of medical science, *penicillin* gets its name from Latin *penicillum*, paint-brush, pencil, a diminutive of *peniculus*, brush, itself a diminutive of *penis*, which means tail. The fungi in *penicillin* are shaped like microscopic pencils.

The word *pen* is not related, but is from Latin *penna*, feather, since of course all early *pens* were sharpened quills. Our historic-minded Supreme Court in Washington has neatly pointed quill *pens*, standing in a vase of shot, on the Bench.

person

In Latin of classic Rome, a *persona* was a mask used by a player; later, it designated the actor himself or the character portrayed. The word is generally thought to be related to *personare*, to sound through, as the voice came through the mouth-opening in the mask worn by all actors, the *dramatis personæ*.

It was not till many centuries later that *person* came to mean a human being in general, a rational creature, as distinguished from animals or things.

Parson is from the same root, and in medieval Latin meant the rector of a parish. Because clergymen wear black coats, *parson* has been added to the name of many animals or birds with black fur or markings. The Isle of Wight *parson* is a cormorant; there is a black-coated *parson rabbit*; and the great black-backed gull is the *parson gull*.

petard

When I heard people say: "He was hoist by his own petard," I always pictured a *petard* as some part of a knight's armor by which he injudiciously got himself hung up. Shakespeare, in *Hamlet*, writes: "For tis the sport to have the enginer Hoist with his owne petar"; and Shakespeare evidently knew his etymology better than I, since *petar* was a Spanish word for a kind of artillery, a small engine of war used to blow in a door or gate. It was a box charged with powder and fired by a fuse, a sort of early *grenade* (or pomegranate). The derivation of *petar* is Latin *pettus*, to break wind, or fart.

picayune

In French Louisiana, as late as the early 18th century, an old copper coin of the Piedmont in France was in circulation. This was, in French, *picaillon*; in Louisiana dialect, *picayune*. The Spanish half-real, valued at 6¼ cents or 3 pence, was also called a *picayune*, as was later a very slim U.S. silver 5-cent piece. These can still be picked up in antique shops on Royal Street in New Orleans. The famous New Orleans newspaper *The Picayune*, my alma mater, was bought with this coin.

To call a person or thing *picayune* is a contemptuous way of saying he or it is small, mean, insignificant. The ultimate origin of the word is obscure, but it may be related to Spanish *pequeño*, little, and Portuguese *pequenino*, tiny, from which we get, via West Indian Negro talk, *pickaninny*, a little one, a child, a word used in places as far-flung as the West Indies, southern United States, South Africa, and Australia. The lowest opinion you can express of anyone in the South is to say: "He's not worth a picayune."

pillar to post

When you run "from pillar to post," from one pursuit or aim to another without any clear purpose, you are using a very old expression that arose in manège, in horsemanship. The *pillar* is the center of the riding ring, and the *posts* are the columns at equal distances, placed two and two around the circumference of the ring. Another authority traces the term to the tennis court and says the original phrase was "toss from post to pillar." It is found, in Lydgate's *Assembly of Gods*, as early as *circa* 1420: "Thus fro poost to pylour he was made to daunce."

pink of perfection

This does not refer to the sanguine, rosy cheeks of health, but *pink* in this phrase means the acme, the top, from Welsh *pwnc*, a point. Shakespeare, in *Romeo and Juliet*, speaks of "the pink of courtesy." From the same root we get *to pink* in fencing—to stab or prick your opponent; and *pinking shears*, which cut cloth into points. The verb *pique* is a French form, meaning stab, sting, stimulate your senses, irritate by jabbing sharply. A *piquant* sauce or girl affects you that way. The etymology of *pink*, as a flower of the Dianthus tribe, is obscure, but some think the name derives from the "pinked" or jagged petals.

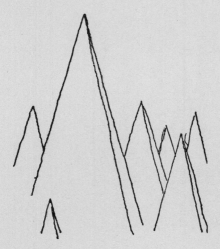

pinnace

This small, light vessel, generally two-masted, and schooner-rigged, often used as a tender for a larger sailing vessel, derived its name from the lumber of which it was built—Latin *pinus*, pine tree.

Corvette, in the modern British navy a light, fast, armored cruiser, derives from Latin *corbis*, basket, because it was originally a slow-sailing old basket of a freighter.

portfolio

This fancy name for a brief-case or an artist's picture-folder comes from two Latin words, *portare*, to carry, and *folium*, leaf. You carry leaves of paper in it. *Foliage* is from the same root, as are *porter*, one who carries; *deportment*, how one carries oneself; *transport*, carry across; *report*, carry back; *deport*, carry out; *import*, carry in; *important*; *portage*; and *portable*. Portmanteau, an old-fashioned word for a piece of luggage, is from the French, and was originally an officer who carried a prince's mantle. *Portmanteau words*, such as "brunch," where breakfast and lunch are packed up together, were invented by Lewis Carroll, who used them brilliantly in *The Hunting of the Snark*.

prestige

Without the desire of every man or woman in the public eye for *prestige*, the modern profession of public relations counsel would be without clients. *Prestige* now means your reputation or influence, based on character, association, and achievement, and containing the quality of dazzling glamor.

But its origin, etymologically, was far from admirable. A French word, *prestige*, in the 16th century meant an illusion, deceit, imposture, juggling tricks, derived from the Latin plural *prestigiæ*. The Latin *præstringere oculos* meant to blindfold, hence to dazzle the eyes or fool the spectator.

A *prestidigitator* is a conjuror who is quick or nimble with the fingers.

prevaricate

This word, now used only in a figurative sense—that of deviating from straightforwardness, to act or speak evasively, to quibble—has its origin in a literal physical act. It is derived from Latin *prævaricare*, meaning to spread the legs apart in a straddle. *Varus* means bent or knock-kneed. The plowman who *prevaricated* made crooked ridges, deviated from the straight furrows in his field. Ranken, writing a *History of France* in 1801, says: "They were careful not to prevaricate, or make crooked serpentine ridges." The figurative sense of *prevaricate* comes from card-playing and the use of *shuffling* to confuse your adversary, not just to mix the cards equitably. *Shuffle* also means to walk askew, to deviate from the true line, from a Teutonic root *skuf-*.

p's and q's

The origin of the admonition "Mind your p's and q's" is uncertain, but there is one story that explains it picturesquely if unauthoritatively. In the reign of Louis XIV, when wigs of unwieldy size were worn and bows were low and formal, two things were required of a courtier—a step forward with the feet, and a low bend of the body. In this action the wig often slipped forward or fell off, a courtly embarrassment. The dancing-master, instructing his noble pupils, would caution them to "Mind your p's (*pieds*, feet) and q's (*queues*, wigs)."

A lawyer of my acquaintance, related to me by marriage, claims to have heard another version, originating in the British House of Commons during Question Hour. He says the phrase means "Mind your Parliamentary Questions."

quintessence

Fourteenth century French *quinte essence*, from medieval Latin *quinta essentia*, the fifth essence, substance of the heavenly bodies, beyond the four earthly elements. One of the aims of medieval alchemists was the discovery of this element by distillation. They never found it, except in a figurative sense; nor have we. *Quintessence*, as we use it, means the most essential part of any substance, the purest form or manifestation of some quality.

Many words spring from the root *quintus*, fifth—the Dionne *quintuplets*, a musical *quintette*, *quint*, a tax of one-fifth.

quisling

This synonym for a traitor, a fifth-columnist (q.v.), an informer to the enemy occupying your country, a collaborationist, derives from the name of Vidkun Quisling, who was all of those loathsome things. Quisling, born in 1887 in Norway, an army officer of his country, conspired with the Nazis in its seizure early in World War II. His name, now found in the dictionary with a small "q," goes down in history as a common noun for traitor.

repugnant

From Latin *repugnare,* to fight back. *Pugnus* is Latin for
fist. A *repugnant* thing or person is one against which or
whom you fight back, because it or he is distasteful, ob-
jectionable, antagonistic, or just contrary to your likes.
Other words from the same root are: *pugilist,* one who
fights with his fists; *pugnacious,* a quarrelsome attitude
found in those quick to pick a fight; and *impugn,* to attack
or assault, figuratively, a reputation. *Pug,* as a dog or a
turned-up nose, seems unrelated, and of obscure origin,
though prizefighters frequently come out of a fight with
such a nose.

restaurant

In French, *restaurer* means to restore, from Latin *restaurare*, to repair, or what we do to ourselves when we enter a *restaurant* for a meal. The earlier use of *restaurant* was in the sense of a strengthening diet, full of vitamins. The current sense was first used in Paris around 1765. One who runs a *restaurant* is a *restaurateur*.

ritzy

American slang for anything lavish, elegant, expensive. In
every capital city of the Western world, almost, there is a
Ritz Hotel, elegant, luxurious, high-priced, and matching
in excellence. Occasionally there is a Ritz that only tries
to be all these superlatives. The original Ritz, on Picca-
dilly, in London, was founded by César Ritz, Swiss restaurateur and hotel-keeper, who lived a long and busy life
from 1850 to 1918. *To ritz* a person is to behave snob-
bishly and superciliously toward him. (*Supercilious*—literally to raise the eyebrows.)

rodomontade

This fine, rolling word, meaning vainglorious boasting, comes from Italian *rodomontada*, a term coined from the name of the Saracen braggart Rodomonte in Ariosto's *Orlando Furioso*, written in the early 16th century. Skeat suggests that the origin was Lombard dialect *rodare*, to turn about, from Latin *rota*, wheel, and *monte*, a mountain—in other words, a tall-tale teller who spins mountains as if they were wheels. *Rodomontade* was used as early as 1612 by Donne in his *Letters*.

romance

Romance and *romantic* had nothing to do, in their origin, with June, moon, girl, boy, or love. Both words derive from popular Latin *Romanice scribere,* to write in the Roman vernacular, as distinguished from literary Latin. In Old French, an epic narrative written in everyday language was a *roman,* and in Middle English a *romaunt.* The *Romance languages,* native-born (*vernacular*), are those derived from vernacular Latin: French, Provençal, Italian, Spanish, Portuguese, Rumanian, etc. The early *romances* were tales in verse, generally about some hero of chivalry, and only incidentally about his love for fair lady.

rubber

The etymology of *a rubber*, as in bridge, is uncertain, but it has no connection with either a "rubber" on a pencil or with a masseur who rubs you down. The word was originally used in bowling, and meant the additional decisive game you rolled to settle a tie match, and it was then "a rubbers." In 1599, Porter, in *The Angry Woman of Abingdon*, wrote: "Weele to the greene to bowles . . . Phillip, come, a rubbers, and so leave." And Middleton and Dekker (1611) in *Roaring Girl*, say: "When your husband comes from his rubbers in a false alley . . . and his bowls run with a false bias."

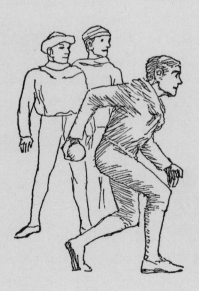

rummage

Schools, churches, and charities nowadays all pick up a little extra money by running *rummage* sales, which at least have one beneficent effect—they clear out attics and storerooms for the cluttered housewife. But *rummage* in its origin had nothing to do with selling that lamp Aunt Bertha gave you for your wedding, and which you always hated. It is from Old French *arrumer*, to arrange the cargo in the hold of a ship. Old French *run* meant the hold, from Anglo Saxon *rūm*, room. The Early English form, *runage*, occurs in connection with stowing wine-casks, and came in with the wine trade from France. The later sense of the word, a turbulent collection of odds-and-ends as in a grab-bag, grew up from the general dragging around and confusion incident to stowing cargo. The *run* was the aftmost part of the ship's hold. The first *rummage sales* were held on the piers to get rid of unclaimed cargo. Hakluyt in his *Voyages*, 1560, wrote: "And that the masters of the ships do looke wel to the romaging."

sabotage

Sabots are great, clumsy wooden shoes, worn by the French peasant in his muddy barnyard, most noisy clackers over cobblestones. The word is somehow related to *savate*, shoe. I believed for years a delightful bit of folk-etymology: to wit, that *sabotage* was a term invented at the time of the French Revolution, when the workers threw a wooden shoe into the works to stall whatever machinery existed in those days (like throwing a monkey-wrench).

The word *sabotage* actually was not invented until about 1910, at the time of the great French railway strikes, and meant, figuratively, to throw a wooden shoe in the gears; deliberate and organized destruction of plant and machinery by dissatisfied workers. The earlier use of the verb *saboter* was to make a noise with *sabots*, to perform badly; e.g., to "murder" a piece of music.

sanguine

From Latin *sanguis*, blood. The early meaning expressed color, blood-red, and is so found in Wyclif: "With . . . blyu vyolet silc, and sanguyn silc." About 1700 the word *sanguinary* developed from *sanguine* (red), meaning causing or delighting in bloodshed; bloody, as "sanguinary wars."

In medieval physiology, one of the four "complexions" or temperaments of man was the *sanguine*—the person with a ruddy complexion, indicative of a courageous, hopeful, and amorous disposition. From this we get our phrase, "of sanguine disposition," which means optimistic, not blood-thirsty.

Related words are *consanguinity*, same blood, kin; *sang royal*, royal blood; *sang-froid*, French, cold blood, unruffled; *sang-de-bœuf*, beef blood, the glowing deep color of old Chinese porcelain; and *sangaree*, a drink of lemon, water, and red wine, via Spanish *sangria*, bleeding.

scandal

From ecclesiastical Latin *scandalum*, a cause of offense or stumbling, a word derived from Greek *skandalon*, snare for an enemy, spring of a trap, believed to be from Indo-germanic *skand-*, to leap or spring. Before the 16th century, the only occurrence of *scandal* in English literature is in the *Ancren Riwle*. After that date, it was used in ecclesiastical writings, and meant specifically discredit to religion caused by the conduct of a priest or of someone looked up to in the community.

By Shakespeare's time, the general sense of rumor injurious to reputation came into use. He wrote, in *A Comedy of Errors*: "I wonder much that you would put me to this shame and trouble, And not without some scandall to your selfe."

In law, *scandal* was the same as *slander*, which derived from Latin *scandalum*, too, through Old French *esclandre*. Slander's twin, *libel*, had no defamatory meaning at first, and meant merely a short writing, from Latin *libellus*, little book.

Scandalize, an entertaining nautical term, is not related, but derives from *scantle*, diminutive of *scant*, short, brief. (Old Norse *skant*). When a sailor "scandalizes the mainsail," he reduces its area by lowering the peak and tricing up the tack.

scruple

When a *scruple*, a small doubt or hesitation, troubles your conscience, it is as if a pebble had hopped into your shoe and made walking just a little uncomfortable. And that is the literal origin of the word, as it comes from Latin *scrupulus*, a little pebble. Cicero used *scruple* figuratively for a cause of uneasiness or anxiety.

Scruple as a small unit of weight, 20 grains on an apothecary's scale, arises from the same stem, since early weights were often pebbles. If you lived in ancient Rome, you might buy two pebbles' worth of whatever the B.C. equivalent was for aspirin—sassafras, perhaps. A 16th-century book on *Physick* says that a "Scruple is twentie barley cornes."

segregation

A word we have heard all too often in relation to minority groups, *segregation* means literally to separate from the flock, hence to set apart, to isolate. (*Isolate* comes from Italian *isola*, from Latin *insula*, island). *Segregate* is derived from the Latin *segrego*, apart from the flock, or separated from your herd of fellow sheep.

When people *congregate* they flock together under the care of a pastor or shepherd. A *gregarious* man loves a big crowd, or flock. An *egregious* fellow or error now is pretty gross and monstrous, and we usually say the word of someone ironically. Originally there was no sense of disparagement, as the prefix *e* or *ex* meant out of the flock, beyond it, in the sense of outstanding, towering over the common run. An *egregious* sheep would once have won a blue ribbon at the fair.

semantics

This new, fashionable, and overworked word, which
means relating to meaning or signification, and about
which scores of books have been written by learned philol-
ogists, comes from Greek *sema*, a mark. *Semantic* means
showing, significant, and its first use was in relation to
signs of the weather. It was never applied to word-mean-
ings until the end of the 19th century. From the same
root we get *semaphore*, mark, bearing, those gay traffic
robots bearing arms shouting stop and go at the traffic.
Phero is Greek for bear. It was *Christopher* who bore
Christ over the stream in his arms.

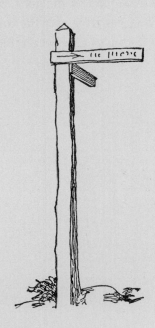

shindig

This is a U.S. colloquialism that, according to Bartlett's 1859 *Dictionary of Americanisms*, comes from "Shin-Dig, a blow on the shins. Southern." It is defined as a dance or party in the "Kentucky Words" section of *American Dialects*. Pretty rough goings-on at those mountaineer dances, down in Al Capp's Li'l Abner country. You needed your shin-guards.

Shindy is an entirely different word, though the meaning is similar to *shindig*. In Smyth's *Sailor's Word-book*, 1867, it is defined as a spree, merrymaking, a dance among seamen. Egan in *Life in London*, 1821, says: "The Jack Tar is quite pleased with his night's cruise, and is continually singing out, 'What a prime Shindy, my Messmates.'"

Simon Pure

When you label something or someone Simon Pure, the real, the genuine, the authentic person or thing, you are using the name of a character in a play. Simon Pure was a Quaker in Mrs. Centlivre's comedy of 1717, *A Bold Stroke for a Wife*, who is impersonated by another character during part of the play. Hence, the real Simon Pure was the genuine article, as distinguished from the pretended.

In my childhood, before the advent of Spry and Crisco, we fried with Simon Pure Leaf Lard, which came in a great bucket.

slave

How tragically topsy-turvy the world is, when the race whose name meant "slave" now are the enslavers of millions. Our word *slave* comes to us, via Old French *esclave*, from the medieval Latin *slavus*, a Slav captive, a common-noun derivative from *Sclavus*, a Slav, itself from late Greek *Sklabos*, a Slavonian, one of the Slavic race captured and made a bondsman.

smart-aleck

Was there a real Aleck who was such a know-it-all, such a would-be clever fellow, that his name got into the language? The reference books have turned up no such man. He could just as well have been smart-Alfred or Archie or Abe. The expression is first used about 1870. Sinclair Lewis, in *The Man Who Knew Coolidge*, writes: "A lot of these smart-aleck cigarette-sucking high-school fraternity yahoos."

Yahoo is, according to *The Tailor and Cutter*, tailors' slang for a crazy, eccentric guy.

soundings

When a mariner ascertains the depth of the water under his keel by means of line and lead, he is taking *soundings*. This word derives from Old English *sund*, which meant water, sea, swimming, and has no relation to Latin *sonus*, audible sound, nor to sound in the sense of healthy, which is from Old English *gesund*, a relative of the German *gesundheit*, politely said to some one who sneezes, to ward off the devil who may gain access at that wide-open moment.

Sound, as an inlet of the sea, is from the same root as *soundings*. Samuel Clemens borrowed his pen-name, Mark Twain, from soundings called out on the Mississippi river steamboats—the second mark on the line. *Sound* in its varying meanings fills five pages in the *Oxford Dictionary*.

Oddly enough, the most modern method of taking soundings, by use of an instrument called a depthometer or fathometer, does depend on sound in the sense of the audible, since it employs radio waves that bounce back from the ocean floor.

squirrel

This charming small beast derives his name from sheer poetry. It comes to us via Latin *sciurus*, from the Greek shadow-tail, *skia*, shade, and *oura*, tail. That gray plume of his is surely a shadow-tail. From the same root *skia* we get a fancy word for shadow-boxing: *sciamachy*. *Sciagraphy* is the science of finding time by shadows, as on a sun-dial; and people in equatorial lands, who cast no shadows when the sun is directly overhead at noon, are *Ascians*. A- is a Greek negative prefix, without.

Star-chamber

Star-chamber proceedings, a trial held in secrecy and with arbitrary powers on the part of the court or investigating body, as in the early disgraceful days of the Dies Committee on Un-American Activities, had its origin during the 14th and 15th centuries in England. During those years, the Lord Chancellor, the Lord Treasurer, justices, and other members of the King's council sat to exercise jurisdiction in an apartment in the royal palace at Westminster. Sir T. Smith in *Commonwealth of England,* 1577, said that the chamber was called *star* "because at the first all the roofe thereof was decked with images of starres gilted."

Because of the tyrannical abuse of its powers by the Court of Star-chamber, under James I and Charles I, it was abolished by an Act of the Long Parliament in 1641. But its name has become proverbial for any arbitrary and oppressive tribunal. There is no authentication for the notion, popularized by Blackstone, that the chamber was the depository of *starrs* or Jewish bonds. *Starr* here is from the Hebrew word *sh'tar*, a writing, and was used in 15th century England for a Jewish bond or release of debt.

stateroom

This U.S. designation for a private cabin on a ship (and now in a Pullman car) started with the elegant gold-and-white luxury of the Mississippi river boats, where each cabin, instead of being numbered, was named for one of the states. I remember traveling once, in my childhood, from Natchez to Vicksburg—on either the *Betsy Ann* or the *Sen. Cordell*—in "Virginia." Of course, the term was used in England for a captain's or superior officer's cabin aboard ship as early as 1660, because Pepys writes in his *Diary* of April 24th: "Very pleasant we were on board the *London* which hath a state-room much bigger than the *Nazeby*, but not so rich."

subterfuge

When you resort to a *subterfuge*, using a device or artifice to escape the force of an argument you cannot counter honestly, you are literally fleeing under cover, since the word comes from Latin *subterfugere*, to flee under. A *subterfuge* may be an evasion, an excuse, a means of escape, or a place of refuge from censure. A *fugitive* is one who flees. *Refugee*, that somber oft-heard word of our times, was first applied to the French Huguenots escaping after the Edict of Nantes in 1685.

From the same root we get *febrifuge*, medicine to make fever fly; *Tempus fugit*, or It's later than you think; and a musical *fugue*, where the little notes fly one after another as if escaping.

suède

This softest of kidskin gets its name from the French **word** for Sweden—*Suède*—and was, at first, used only as descriptive of gloves, French *gants de Suède*.

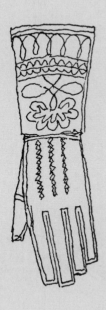

sycophant

This word, which now means servile flatterer, a lickspittle, meant originally an informer or a slanderer. It comes from Greek *sykon*, fig, and *phaino*, to show, a fig-shower, and its etymology is unsatisfactory. One explanation, not substantiated, is that a *sycophant* in Greece was an informer against the unlawful exportation of figs. Another is that it referred to the so-called obscene gesture of "making a fig," French *faire la figue*, which consists in thrusting the thumb between two closed fingers. Fig-tree in Latin is *ficus*. The expression "don't give a fig for it" is one of contempt for the picayune (q.v.) thing mentioned.

tabby–cat

The sleek gray-striped puss called a *tabby* gets her name from an Arabian word, *Attabiy,* a certain quarter of Bagdad where striped silk taffeta was woven. Attab was the great-grandson of Omeyya, famed in Arab legend. A cat was first referred to as a *tabby,* in writing, in 1695. *Tabby* as a nickname for an old maid became associated with *tabby-cat* because both wore gray and had neat and delicate habits of washing and eating, but the use appears earlier than 1695 and may have been a contraction of Tabitha, an old-maidish sounding name.

The 18th-century girls who were too flat-chested for beauty had their "falsies," just as girls do today, but they called them "tabbies." We find this in *Taste,* published in 1752: "Bless me, Mr. Carmine, don't mind my shape this bout; for I am only in jumps. Shall I send for my tabbies?"

tabloid

To most moderns, *tabloid* now means chiefly a newspaper in compressed form. But the word, as a trade mark for concentrated drugs, was invented and registered on March 14, 1884, by Burroughs, Wellcome Co., the British drug manufacturers. The suffix *-oid*, meaning resembling, was added to the root of Latin *tabula*, a flat board, a plank, a board to play cards on, a writing tablet. *Tavern* is probably from the same root, as the first wine-shops were huts built of planks.

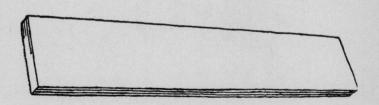

taffrail

Any sailor knows about the *taffrail log,* that spinning fin and meter which indicates knots traveled, and which is fixed to the *taffrail,* or more correctly *aft* rail. It has become *taffrail* through confusion in sound. *Taffrail* was derived from the Dutch *tafereel,* a panel or picture, diminutive of *tafel,* a table, and was originally any carved panel; in a ship, the upper part of the flat portion of the stern above the transom, ornamented, in the great days of sail, with gilded and painted carvings.

tall

This is a word that has changed its meaning entirely. It started life as Old English *getæl*, which meant swift, prompt, ready, active. A *tall* ship may have had high masts, but she was also a fast one. Later, *tall* meant handsome, goodly, brave. "Tall of hand" did not signify big hands but skillful ones. Eventually, the word lost its earlier senses, and meant, as we use it, merely high and lofty. "Tall tales" are so up-in-the-clouds you can't believe them.

A long list of adjectives has gone through a similar shift in sense. *Canny* had at first no suggestion of shrewdness and caution, as in "canny Scot," but meant to know how, to be able. *Clean* at one period in its history meant little, puny (like German *klein*), then reverted to its original meaning of clear and pure. *Cunning* meant knowing, not either sly or cute. *Clever* was related to Middle English *clivers*, claws, talons, clutches, and a clever man was nimble of claw, quick to seize, dexterous, an adjective used about hands but not brains. *Deft*, which now means skillful, dexterous, neat-fingered, is a doublet of *daft* and meant mild, gentle, meek, fit. *Daft*, which originally meant becoming or fit, came to mean mild and innocent, inoffensive, and, eventually, silly and foolish. *Handsome* is another word that, like clever, originally referred to hands. A *handsome* man could be as ugly as sin so long as he handled things cleverly. A *handsome* axe fitted comfortably in the palm of your hand.

Pretty has gone through an even more complete metamorphosis: it meant, at first, in Old English, tricky, deceitful, wily. For several centuries the word dropped out of the language entirely, until, in the 15th century, it reappeared and passed successively from meaning tricky, to clever, to pleasing, to someone or something of moderate beauty.

tatterdemalion

The first element of this word comes from the Scandinavian word for rags, shreds, scraps of cloth. Some wordster took the adjective *tattered* and added a fanciful but unmeaning ending, originally pronounced to rhyme with stallion, as you can hear in this Ben Jonson quotation: "This Horse pictur'd showes that our Tatter-de-mallian Did ride the French Hackneyes and lye with th' Italian."

Another suggested derivation is that *tatter* came from *Tatar*, one of an oriental tribe, later called Tartars. Genghis Khan, in the 13th century, with his wild Tartar horde swept over Asia and Eastern Europe. The Romans changed Tatar to Tartar because they were such barbaric hellions, and the Roman hell was Tartarus. Later, the terror-bearing horde became mere wandering gypsies, or tatterdemalions.

Thespian

Thespis was the traditional father of Greek tragedy, living in the 6th century B.C. Hence, *Thespian* means pertaining to tragedy or, more generally, to the dramatic art, and an actor is a *Thespian*. *Tragedy* comes from Greek *tragos*, goat, and *odos*, singer or song, as in Franz Werfel's play, *Goat Song*, produced by the Theatre Guild in 1921. One theory is that the actors dressed in goat-skins; another, that early drama was religious and ritualistic, centered around the sacrifice of the *scapegoat*, who carried away the sins of man.

The word *scapegoat* was invented by Tindale, in 1530, to express what he believed to be the literal meaning of the Hebrew phrases in Leviticus xvi, 8, 10, 26: "The goote on which the lotte fell to scape." In the ancient ritual of the Day of Atonement, two goats were brought to the temple. One was chosen by lot to be sent away alive into the wilderness (q.v.), bearing away on his back, symbolically, the sins of all the people. This was the *scapegoat*. The other unfortunate beast was offered up in sacrifice. A *scapegrace*, an incorrigible scamp, is one who escapes the grace of God.

tide

When you say—and who doesn't—"time and tide," you are guilty of tautology, because the two words were once synonyms, from the same Old Teutonic root *ti-*, meaning to extend. The *tide* of the sea isn't that miracle of flowing and ebbing water dictated by sun and moon, but actually the fixed *time* of flood and ebb. In the expressions *eventide* and *noontide* we retain the twinship with *time*. *Betide* means to happen.

tirade

A *tirade* is a protracted harangue of abuse or denunciation, a quick volley of bullet-words, and the meaning follows closely the derivation, which was from the Italian *tirata*, a volley, from Latin *tirare*, to draw a bow. The French for free-shooter is *franc-tireur*.

toast

A slice of bread deliciously browned over the fire was, in popular Latin, *tostata*, from classic Latin *torrere*, to parch (like *torrid* as in Zone). How did *toast* come to mean to drink someone's health, to pledge your lady in wine? The *toast*, or slightly burned bread, spiced, was put in the wine to flavor it—hence, to drink a toast. The figurative application is that the name of a chosen lady is supposed to flavor a bumper just as the spiced toast does the drink.

Tom and Jerry

This spiced punch, a favorite tipple at Twenty-One in New York on a chill Christmas Eve, derives its name from the two chief characters in Egan's *Life in London, or Days and Nights of Jerry Hawthorne and his elegant friend Corinthian Tom,* published in 1821. In 1828, a sequel came out—*Finish to the Adventures of Tom, Jerry and Logic.* These dashing young bloods of the Regency were extremely popular, and lent their coupled names not only to a spicy drink but to all sorts of racy doings. To Tom-and-Jerry meant to drink and riot and raise hell. Washington Irving took a high moral tone of disapprobation toward the young gentlemen when he wrote, in *Life and Letters*: "We are too apt to take our ideas of English life from such vulgar sources as Tom and Jerry, and we appear to be Tom and Jerrying it to perfection in New York."

tom-cat

One of the best-sellers in Britain in 1760 was an anonymous work entitled *The Life and Adventures of a Cat,* and the engaging hero was "Tom the Cat," patterned after Caxton's "Tybert the Catte" in his *Reynard the Fox.* The romance commences: "Tom the Cat is born of poor but honest parents." So popular was this puss that every other male cat was christened Tom; and by 1809, *tom,* uncapitalized, had become a generic term. "It's enough to make a tom cat talk French grammar," said Dickens in *Nicholas Nickleby.*

Thomas, incidentally, is derived from the Hebrew word for twin. *Tom,* as a typically masculine name, is used as a generic name for any man. There is a *Tom-fool,* a ridiculous clownish fellow; *Long Tom,* a famous naval gun; big bells like "Tom of Lincoln" and "Tom of Oxford"; *Old Tom,* which is gin; and *Tommy Atkins,* British army equivalent of G.I. Joe.

torture

From the Latin *torquere*, to twist, to torment. A *tortuous* road is a highway full of bends and twists. From the same root we get the legal term a *tort*, meaning injury, right of action for damages; *torsion*, act of twisting a body spirally; and *tortoise*, because of that lethargic creature's crooked or twisted feet. A *torch* was originally made of a hank of tow, twisted and dipped in pitch. According to Pliny, the *nasturtium* was so named because its pungent smell twists the nose. See *flower*.

That thin and rubbery corn-meal cake of Mexico, the *tortilla*, is not related to this root "to twist," but is a diminutive of the Spanish *torta*, cake, which comes from Latin *tortam panis*, a cake of bread. *Torso*, which sounds related, is from still another derivation: the Greek *Thyrsus* or wand of Bacchus, a stem.

Tory

I have always marveled that the British Labour candidates are too gentlemanly in their campaign speeches to use the derivation of *Tory*. It is from Irish *tóraidhe*, pursuer. In the 17th century, a tory (small "t") was one of the dispossessed Irish, who became outlaws, living by plundering and killing the English settlers and soldiers; a *bog-trotter*, a *rapparee* (a man who carries a rapier). In 1679–80, Tory with a capital T became a nickname given by the Exclusioners to those who opposed the exclusion of James, Duke of York (a Roman Catholic) from the succession to the crown.

After 1689, *Tory* became the name of one of the two great political parties in Britain. The opposing party, the *Whigs*, perhaps got this name as a shortening of *whiggamore*, a body of insurgents of the west of Scotland who in 1648 marched on Edinburgh, their expedition being called the "whiggamore raid." A *whig* was a country bumpkin, and *more* was a mare—a kind of Scottish beggar-on-horseback. *Tantivy*, an echoic word representing the sound of a horse's feet galloping, was another nickname applied to a Tory because of a caricature published in 1680. This picture showed a group of High Church clergymen mounted on the Church of England and "riding tantivy" to Rome, behind the Duke of York.

trance

This word comes to us from the Latin prefix *trans*, across, and the verb *ire*, to go, via Old French *transe*, which was the passage across from life to death, according to the 12th-century St. Alexis. It also carried the sense of dread or apprehension of coming evil. A medium who goes into a *trance* is suspended on the bridge between consciousness and unconsciousness. This modern meaning, as in a hypnotic state, was used by Chaucer: "And longe tyme he lay forth in a traunce." If you are *entranced* by the beauty of dogwood in spring or by the acting of Jean Arthur as Peter Pan, you are in a trance, hypnotized.

tribulation

If, like Job, you are oppressed by trials and *tribulations*, you are beaten like grain in the threshing, since this word is derived from Latin *tribulare*, to press down, to afflict, from *tribulum*, a threshing-sledge, a grinding-machine. Poetic if painful. A species of poll-tax formerly levied on tin miners in Cornwall was called *tribulage*. *Tribulation* was, in Shakespeare's day, a cant word for a gang of disturbers. He writes, in *Henry VIII*: "These are the youths that thunder at the Playhouse . . . that no Audience but the tribulation of Tower Hill, or the Limbes of Limehouse, their deare Brothers, are able to endure."

Tuxedo

When your dinner-party hostess writes on her invitation: "Black tie," you climb into your Tuxedo feeling elegant and partified, little knowing that the word means "round-footed." This is what the Algonkin Indians contemptuously called the Wolf Tribe of the Delawares when they hunted and fought in what is now Orange County, N.Y.

The Lorillard family later on succeeded the Indians as owners of Tuxedo Lake and Park, which became a resort for the fashionable. In the 1880's the Tuxedo Club was founded, and here Griswold Lorillard is said to have worn the first tailless dinner jacket or *tuxedo*.

The origin of the name of the *swallowtail* coat is so obvious that you forget it is a lovely metaphor unless you happen to see a flock of swallows, as I did recently in Gibson Island Harbor, Maryland. We were peacefully at anchor on our sloop at sundown, when a ballroomful of swallows, each fashionable and trim in his pointed *swallowtail*, settled merrily on our boom. They looked extremely elegant with pinkish buff vests to set off the severe black of their coats.

uncouth

This word did not originally mean awkward and uncultured in manners and language, but merely unknown, since it comes to us from an Old English word *uncouth*, not known, itself from a Gothic word. At first, it was used about unfamiliar paths, places, lands, things and people who were alien. In the 16th century, the insular English felt anything strange must be unseemly and indecorous; so gradually the word took on the meaning of wild and uncultured, just as the Athenian Greeks considered strangers who could not speak their language barbarians.

The word *barbarian* was an imitation of stammering, un-Hellenic speech. (*Barbara* is a lovely name; but do parents really want their little daughters to be wild savages?)

We rarely use the positive word *couth*, which means known, familiar, snug, cosy. An obsolete legal term for a person knowingly harboring an outlaw is *couthutlaughe*.

uranium

This rare metallic element, found in pitchblende and first mentioned in 1797, is now important to the world because of its necessity in making the A-bomb. The origin of its name is not frighteningly destructive at all, as it comes from *Uranus*, the planet, in Greek mythology the husband of Gæa, Earth Goddess, and father of Cronos or Saturn.

very

This small, overworked word, now used in a haphazard fashion to intensify almost every adjective, had its origin in the stem of Latin *verus*, meaning true. In its more careful use, *very* still means true or exact, really or truly entitled to the name or designation given, possessing the true character of the person or thing named. We preserve this sense in the phrase "my very own."

From the same stem we have: *veracious*, speaking the truth; *verify*, make true, prove by good evidence; *verily*, in truth; *verdict*, true words; and *verisimilitude*, likeness to truth.

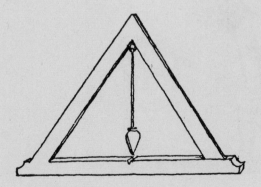

vestige

This word comes from Latin *vestigium*, a footstep, a footprint, a trace or mark you leave when you walk in soft earth. Our modern use is therefore poetic and figurative— a mark or trace or visible sign of something not now present, like a *vestigial* organ in the body. When we say: "There's not a vestige of truth in the rumor," we mean not a scrap, not a particle, not even a footprint. The F.B.I., when it *investigates* a person, tracks down his footsteps.

virus

I was laid extremely low this spring by what is fashionably called *Virus X*, though my doctor witheringly said the malady was nothing more (nor less) than old-fashioned flu or grippe. *Virus* is the Latin word for slimy liquid, poison, offensive odor or taste, and was first described about 1400 in *Lanfranc's Cirurgie* as "a thin venomy quitter"; though why "quitter" I can't imagine, since it clung to me a full month. A *virus* may be the venom emitted by a poisonous snake, or by a poison-pen.

Virulent may be used of a disease of violent malignancy, or of bitter and spiteful writing, as produced by Westbrook Pegler in his column. Its antidote lies in the sandwiching words in the dictionary: *virtuousness*, which precedes *virulence*; and *vis*, or strength, energy, vigor, which follows it on the page.

La Grippe was first used in France, about 1776, for the epidemic cold, because it gripped the victim in his throat and limbs. *Influenza* is a much earlier term for the same ill, known as early as 1504, but in 1743 applied specifically to the epidemic of *la grippe* which spread from Italy to all Europe. Hence the Italian word, *influenza*, meaning "to flow in."

I believe the three great enemies of mankind are rust, moths, and the common cold.

volcano

Another of those words, frequent in English, derived from a proper name. The fire-spouting mountain is fittingly named after the Roman god of fire, *Vulcanus*, son of Jupiter and Juno, husband of Venus. He had his forges under Mount Ætna, with consequences all too fiery for generations of Sicilians, who hope Vulcan will go easy on the bellows in future. Vulcan was architect, smith, armorer, chariot-builder, and artist of all work in Olympus. He built the houses of the gods of brass, their golden airtreading shoes, and he shod the celestial steeds. Nowadays he repairs tires for terrestrial steeds known as automobiles, when we *vulcanize* the rubber.

wan

This word, which now means pale, started life as just the opposite. An Old English word, it meant dark, gloomy, black. Since such sable hues depressed the spirits, making people feel sad and dismal, causing palor, *wan* took on the present sense of pallid, faded, sickly. Chaucer, in *Troylus*, wrote: "He for wo was pale and wan"; and Sir John Suckling asked: "Why so pale and wan, fond lover?"

wanton

The current use of this word, as a noun, means a lascivious and lewd woman. (Why is it never used of a man? That old double standard, I suppose.) But originally, *wanton* meant merely undisciplined. It comes from the Middle English *towen*, meaning to train, with the negative prefix *wan-*, *wantowen*. An antonym, long lost to use, was *wel-itowen*, well-brought-up, the disciplined child in contrast to the *wanton* one.

Wanton means given to amorous dalliance; but it also means sportive, jovial, free, unrestrained, as Shakespeare used it in A *Midsummer Night's Dream*: "When we have laught to see the sailes conceive, And grow big bellied with the wanton wind."

wretch

This word is derived from Old Saxon *wrekkio*, a term applied to the Magi, which in turn came from Old High German *reccheo*, meaning exile, adventurer, knight errant; and ultimately from the Teutonic stem *wrak-*, which is the origin of our verb *wreak*. It is interesting that the German *recke* means warrior or hero, while *wretch*, from the same stem, means quite the opposite—one sunk in misfortune, a hapless being. Originally, a *wretch* was a person banished from his native country, an exile; hence, since no one is more lost than a refugee, any creature drowned in distress. At times, *wretch* means a vile or despicable person; and at times, playfully, deprecatingly, a little creature, as when Shakespeare in *Romeo and Juliet* says: "The pretty wretch lefte crying." Or Shelley in *Hellas*: "Swift as the radiant shapes of sleep From one whose dreams are paradise Fly, when the fond wretch wakes to weep."

yarn

From Anglo-Saxon *gearn*, thought to come from an Aryan root containing the idea of winding which appears in Old Norse *görn*, entrails, and also in Latin *haruspex*, one who divines by looking at the entrails of beasts. Thus from a wound-up ball of worsted we come to the figurative sense of a sailor's long tale. While seamen spun their *yarns* of incredible adventure, they were usually busy at some sedentary job such as yarn-twisting for rope or caulking. There is a secondary allusion to the length of the story. *Yachting* magazine prints monthly an entertaining page called "Under the Lee of the Longboat," by Spun Yarn.

yclept

This is a facetious and make-believe Old English way of saying "called, named, styled so-and-so." The prefix *y-* was used in Middle English to form past participles, and here is part of *ycleped*, called out. Elizabethan poets used *yclept* as an affected literary archaism, and *yclepts* run riot in the various versions of the King Arthur tales, from Mark Twain to Howard Pyle. Other uses of the prefix *y-* were *yblent*, blinded; *yblest*, blessed; *yborn*; *ybound*; *ybrent*, burnt; *yclad*, clothed; *ycore*, chosen; *ydight*, dressed—and so on through the alphabet.

ye

When the New England teashop proprietress—or licensed victualer, as we call them in Nantucket—goes all quaint on us and hangs out a shingle announcing Ye Olde Tea Shoppe, she thinks she is being very Olde Englishe. But in simon-pure (q.v.) Anglo-Saxonry, this Y was merely the archaic way of writing "the." There was a dipththong in Anglo-Saxon called "thorn" and written thus: þ, pronounced "th." When carelessly written, the loop at the top was left open, making the resemblance to Y. The only legitimate *ye* is the old plural of "you."

zenith

This comes from the Arabic *Samt-ar-ras*, literally way or path overhead, and it means just that: the point of the sky directly overhead. In astronomy, the *zenith* is also the point of the horizon at which a heavenly body arises. Figuratively, you reach the *zenith* of your career or of your happiness when you arrive at the climax, the culmination, the highest point. In *The Tempest* Shakespeare wrote: "I finde my Zenith doth depend upon A most auspitious starre."

The opposite of *zenith* is *nadir*, from the Arabic *es-samt*, the way directly under one's feet; hence, figuratively, the lowest tide of depression. *Azimuth* is another word from the same Arabic root. To astronomers and navigators, the *azimuth* of a star is an arc of the horizon, measured from some fixed point (North or South) to a point beneath the star.

zest

The origin of this word is obscure, but it originally meant a piece of lemon peel, such as we put in a Martini, to give piquancy (q.v.) to some food or drink. Figuratively, *zest* imparts relish or savor to whatever you are doing. Dickens, in *Dombey and Son*, says: "The Native had private zests and flavours on a side-table, with which the Major daily scorched himself." Perhaps Major Grey's chutney? While the English thought of *zest* as lemon or orange peel, the French defined it as "the thicke skin, or filme whereby the kernell of a wall-nut is divided," which they used for flavoring.

Index of Words and Phrases

A NOTE ON THE TYPE

This book was set on the Linotype in ELECTRA, *designed by W. A. Dwiggins. The Electra face is a simple and readable type suitable for printing books by present-day processes. It is not based on any historical model, and hence does not echo any particular time or fashion. It is without eccentricities to catch the eye and interfere with reading — in general, its aim is to perform the function of a good book printing-type: to be read, and not seen.*

Typographic and binding designs are by W. A. Dwiggins.

The book was composed by The Plimpton Press, Norwood, Massachusetts. Printed and bound by The Book Press, Brattleboro, Vt.